TODDLER TALKING

BOOST YOUR CHILD'S LANGUAGE
AND BRAIN DEVELOPMENT
IN THREE EASY STEPS

VICTORIA ANG-NOLASCO, MD
Foreword by Alexis L. Reyes, MD

Toddler Talking: *Boost Your Child's Language and Brain Development in Three Easy Steps*

Publisher:
Hatch and Grow Inc.
G/F Total Mabini Office Building corner Mabini-San Sebastian Street
Barangay 33, Bacolod City, Philippines
hatchandgrow.org

Toddler Talking —1st edition
ISBN: 978-1-64775-616-1 (Paperback)
ISBN: 978-1-64775-615-4 (eBook)

Book Interior and E-book Design by Amit Dey | amitdey2528@gmail.com
Edited by: Lisa P. Turner, D.Sc. | https://turnercreekpublishing.com/
Cover design by Angie of @pro_ebookcovers

For Johnson and Jake
Who gave me the courage and inspiration to write

For my mom
Who lovingly practiced what's in this book even
before researchers discovered it

For my dad
Whose tales made story time amazing
And who I wish were still around today to share them

For my mentors and colleagues
This book is your work, too

For the kids and parents I've worked with
I'm writing this for you

This book comes with an online resource library.
Get it now at toddlertalkingbook.com.

ALSO BY
VICTORIA ANG-NOLASCO, MD

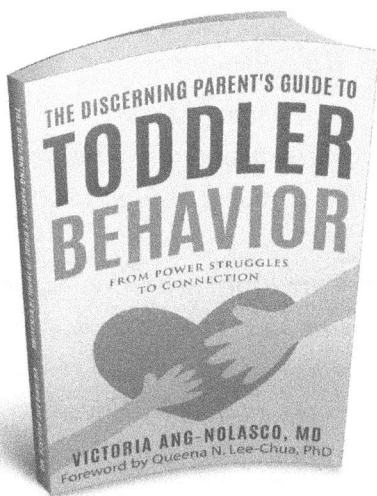

TABLE OF CONTENTS

FOREWORD

Alexis L. Reyes, MD

I AM PROUD TO write this.

After all, "Toyang," as she is fondly called, poured a lot of time and hard work to what will be a wonderful addition to the lack of essential readings on "toddlerhood." I am certain that every parent, pediatrician, developmental pediatrician, or child advocate for that matter would want a copy of this. As a developmental pediatrician myself, I do not have all the right answers about an age that is amazing but challenging as well.

I am not surprised that Toyang wrote this for her son but for others too.

The harsh realities of these past two years were enough to isolate most of us but were not able to prevent the "slow-release" of deep-seated insights which would have been taken for granted in the "old normal." Yes, there is always a silver lining, and I am glad that Toyang saw this and did something about it. She eloquently talks about the science and the art of child development in words that everyone can understand. The unfolding of events, the reasons why these happen, the consequences of behavior that led to what we recognize in the template of "toddlerhood" was written for all those who will appreciate practical and thoughtful advice.

I am happy to be part of this endeavor and slightly jealous.

This is by no means an "encyclopedia" or bible but a practical guide so that those who feel helpless and tired can sit back, read a few pages and be mindful that their children are little miracles. Soon enough, the age of toddlerhood will lead to better, remarkable lives. Until then, I would spend it wisely like Toyang did.

I am proud of you.
Ninang Alexis

Alexis L. Reyes, MD is the pioneer Developmental and Behavioral Pediatrician in the Philippines and one of the founders of the International Developmental Pediatrics Association. She has spent over the past three decades helping and advocating for children and their families. The developmental pediatricians she has trained and mentored have gone on to practice all over the country. She has also published multiple books and researches advancing the field of developmental and behavioral pediatrics.

INTRODUCTION

Why this Book, and Why Now?

IN THIS BOOK, you'll learn how to boost your child's brain and language development in three easy steps. I share what scientific research tells us, and how you can use this research to your advantage at home.

When do children start talking? Should I worry if my child isn't talking yet? What can I do to help my baby or toddler learn to talk? These are just some of the questions we'll answer in this book.

I often hear parents ask:

- My one-year-old hasn't said any words yet, not even "mama." At that age, my niece could already say "ball" and "book". Should I worry?
- My eighteen-month-old isn't talking yet. Everyone says to wait until he goes to school, and he will catch up and start talking. They say it's too early to see a doctor about it. Is this true, or do I need to seek a professional?
- My two-year-old seems to understand what I say, but he's not yet talking. What should I do?
- Does my toddler need to learn reading and math?

- My son can name colors, vehicles and dinosaurs. But he doesn't tell me when he needs something. We have to guess. Is this normal?

To add to all the uncertainty, from the moment people find out a mom is pregnant, she immediately receives an onslaught of parenting advice. A lot of this advice is conflicting:

- Just let your child play vs. Your child is being unproductive. Teach the alphabet now!
- No screen time for babies vs. My baby became smarter watching YouTube.
- You should respond when your baby cries vs You're spoiling him.

When I was a new parent, this deluge of comments was enough to make me want to hide in a remote mountain and get food and baby supplies dropped by helicopter, Hunger Games style.

Unfortunately, a lot of what we hear about parenting and child development is based on myth. These myths add to the stress and overwhelm of being a parent. No matter how hard we try, we still feel as if we can't get this parenting thing right.

There's always someone telling us we're doing something wrong. A relative or even a stranger sees our child crying and clicks her tongue in disapproval. A post on our Instagram feed points out yet *another* thing we should do, but we don't really have time for. We hear about everything people say we should do, and we feel guilty.

I get it. I totally understand where you're at. When I became a parent, I questioned what I was doing. I'd get "shiny object syndrome" every time I read about some program or method. It was what I'd learned from my professional training vs the marketing messages on the internet.

- Babies do learn to use gestures as part of everyday life, right? Why are many parents now made to feel they are missing out if they don't formally teaching sign language to their babies?
- All those "toddler activities" with multiple materials to prepare and twenty steps to follow—does my one-year-old really need them?
- Aren't beads choking hazards? Why are they in "sensory kits" that are being marketed as "must have" items for baby and toddler play?
- We don't really need to do flash cards and letter-a-week drills with a two-year-old, right?
- Do we now expect kids to read at age 2 and write at age 3?

Fortunately, I have several mentors to guide me—experienced developmental pediatricians and parents whose children are now capable adults. It turns out our training was right all along. The science is there, telling us what to do. And what science actually says is not as hard as what the internet tells us to do.

I wanted others to learn from my experience, so I began writing about child development and parenting. Then I started getting feedback from parents.

"Thanks so much. It makes so much sense, but it's the first time I heard this!"

"I felt the pressure lightening up. This is an answered prayer for me."

"I wish I had known this even before I gave birth."

"More people need to hear about this."

Because of all the mixed messages parents get, what felt like common knowledge to us as developmental pediatricians was actually a stunning revelation for parents. I realized how there's the need to translate the scientific research in a way that empowers parents to make the transformation from confused to confident, from stressed to joyful.

That's why I wrote this book.

As I write this, we've been through more than two years of the COVID pandemic. Our babies and toddlers have never known a world where you could go anywhere or meet up with anyone without any worries of being exposed to the virus. Masks and hand sanitizer—which I never considered a necessity until I entered medical school—are now a way of life even for our young kids.

Among the first words my child learned—along with "ice cream," "let's play," and "wash hands"—were "virus," "COVID-19," and "social distancing."

Although restrictions have been loosening lately, our kids are still not getting the same in-person experiences they did before. A lot of the help and options available to us are out of the picture for now. Parents are completely exhausted and burned out. Kids are having more mental health and behavior problems. Now, more than ever, we need support on getting through these challenges in the early years.

I hope this book will help provide the support you need, and that it becomes a part of your everyday life as a family. Refer to it often.

Keep coming back to this book as your baby grows older. Share this book with your family and with others who help you take care of your child.

Then let me know how your parenting journey turns out.

Who This Book is For

Are you worried about how to give your baby the best start in life?

Do you feel exhausted keeping up with everything people say you need to do as a parent?

Are you tired of people comparing your child with someone else? ("His cousin can already recite the alphabet! Why can't he?")

Do you want to save time and effort by focusing on what research has shown to work, instead of constantly trying one thing after another?

Are you ready to truly connect with your child, and feel less stress and more calm as a parent?

If any of these resonate with you, you'll love this book.

If you're the parent of a baby or toddler, and you want to make the most out of this critical time in your child's development, this book is for you.

Maybe you're expecting a baby, or you have a new baby. Or you already have a one-, two-, or even a three-year-old. You want to bring out the best in your little one.

Or you already have concerns about your child's speech and language development. You want to know what your next steps should be.

You're busy. You don't have a lot of time. You want a guide that's straight to the point. No fluff.

You also want science-backed methods that respect your child's development, and what stage she's in.

If these sound like what you need, you're in the right place. You're exactly the person I had in mind while I was writing this book.

If your child has speech delay or has special needs, this book isn't a substitute for getting an assessment and the interventions recommended by your doctor. Don't worry, I've included a practical guide on what to do if you think your child might have speech delay, so you don't feel lost.

Who This Book is NOT For

This book is not for you if you don't believe that simple, science-backed ways can work. If you think that only complicated and fancy programs can get results, this isn't for you.

This book isn't for you if you just want to plant your child in front of a screen so he will learn, or give some magic supplement or milk formula to "make him smart."

Child development doesn't work that way. There *is* what I like to call a "parenting magic wand," and I'll talk about it later. But there's no magic supplement or program.

Parents have to be involved. And by "involved," I don't mean spending hours printing out worksheets and preparing activities. I mean actually *being* with our kids. You'll see how this is easier that all the things that the internet tells us we should do.

Why This Book is Different

It's based on science

This book is based on what we currently know about brain science and child development. In the past ten years, what we know about the brains of babies and young kids has expanded dramatically.

When I tell parents about these discoveries—like how unexpectedly simple it is to help babies and young kids learn—many are shocked. That's because it's quite different what from parents often hear.

A lot of the parenting advice out there is based on opinion. You see an advertisement for a "proven" method, and by "proof", they mean testimonials from people who've tried it. Testimonials and reviews are great for, say, deciding where to eat or which diaper bag to buy.

But science isn't a popularity contest. We can't just take a bunch of stories and call that proof. There's an actual scientific process. Unfortunately, the findings from solidly conducted research are often buried in thick textbooks, medical journals and jargon-filled conferences.

My aim for this book is to make these evidence-based strategies easy to understand and practical to implement.

It's based on how young brains actually work

The methods in this book work with your child's brain and not against it. Often we're told to do things that go against what toddler brains are designed to do.

For example, I'd say up to 80 percent of "toddler activities" on the internet aren't really toddler activities. They're actually activities for older kids, repackaged and marketed to parents of toddlers.

However, you can't take the methods used to teach an older child (such as reading or math lessons) and use them to make a baby or toddler "advanced." We need to consider the child's readiness and developmental stage.

When there's a mismatch between what we try to do and the child's developmental level, parenting will be a constant struggle. But if we work with your child's brain instead and do what is developmentally appropriate, we'll be setting up you and your child for success.

It's practical and easy to implement as a busy parent

I feel you. I know what it's like to be completely exhausted by 9:00. AM. *Not* pm. To juggle at least three simultaneous demands on your attention at any one time—your toddler, your work meeting, a family member who wants you to do something. To collapse into bed at 10 pm, all the while knowing your day isn't over and you still have a to-do list to tackle.

Sadly, it can be our kids' language development that gets pushed to the back burner.

What if I told you that even as a busy parent, you *can* build your baby or toddler's language skills. Right now. Not when you have hours of uninterrupted time. Because, let's face it, "uninterrupted time" will never happen. Well, maybe after your youngest child turns 21 . . . .

That's why in this book you'll learn how to support your child's language development in the middle of those crazy days. Even if you only have exactly two and a half minutes to scan this book until your child starts yelling "Mamimamimamimammy! MAAH-HHMEEEE!!!!" at the top of his lungs.

I combined what science has shown to work with what's practical in our daily lives. And I've personally seen the results in families I've worked with, and in my own child at home.

So that when we feel very, very tired, and we barely have any energy left—we know where to focus that last bit of energy. We know what will truly be the most effective. What will matter most to our kids in the long run.

That's also why this book does not have a "lesson plan" or a "curriculum" to follow. Because we're parents. While we're our kids' first teachers, we're not a school. And that's a good thing! Your toddler does not need you to be a school.

Also, while "toddler homeschooling" curriculums are popular on the internet, there's no evidence they actually help at this age. But the methods in this book, which are simpler, easier and more practical, are the methods that do have evidence behind them.

Notes on the use of certain words

In this book, I alternate "he/him" and "she/her." Whichever pronoun was used in a particular sentence, it will apply regardless of gender.

Also, we usually prefer to use the word "neurotypical" instead of "normal."

If your child does not fit the description of "neurotypical," in no way is it a criticism of your child or your parenting. Rather, this book celebrates diversity and advocates respect and appreciation for all kids, regardless of where they may be in the spectrum of child development.

PART I

How Your
Child Learns to Talk

CHAPTER 1

WHAT IS LANGUAGE? WHY IT'S NOT ABOUT NAMING FLASH CARDS

> *"Children are born wired for feelings and ready to learn...*
> *Children are active participants in their own development."*
>
> **—Dr. Jack Schonkoff, From Neurons to Neighborhoods:**
> **The Science of Early Childhood Development.**

MANY PEOPLE THINK that building toddler language skills is all about teaching kids to recite the alphabet, name objects on flash cards, know shapes and colors, or memorize nursery rhymes.

But language is much more than that. The technical definition of language is "the symbolic and systematic communication system through which humans share ideas, thoughts, emotions and beliefs."[1]

This tells us two things:

1. Language is used to communicate and interact with others.
2. Language is a system that has many components.

---

[1] Feldman and Messick. 2009. "Language and Speech Disorders," *Developmental-Behavioral Pediatrics*, 4th ed.

What Toddler Language is All About

The priority during the toddler years is to learn *interactive language*. This means **communicating with others, and not merely reciting something by rote.**

Even as a newborn, your baby is already starting to learn language. She may not understand the words yet, but she's getting to know you and the world around her.

> The priority during the toddler years is to learn interactive language.

When you talk with your baby and smile at her, or when you play peek-a-boo and tell her stories—these are her first "language lessons."

Most people don't realize it, but these are all examples of language:

- Your baby looks at you when you call him.
- Your toddler greets her cousin, whether it's by waving or saying hi. Or maybe she invented her own greeting.
- When talking with you, your child knows how to take turns speaking and listening. He pauses and listens when you say something.

These are part of language learning, and they're more important than memorizing the alphabet!

What's Included in Learning to Talk

When pediatricians see a child in the clinic, an important part of the consult is observing the child and how he communicates.

It's not just how many words a child is able to say. We also note whether a child uses the words correctly, when it's appropriate to say them.

We observe the child's voice (such as tone and volume), gestures, eye contact, and body language. In addition to looking at each of these individually, we also look at how well a child coordinates these different aspects of communication.

For example, a very important skill we look for is *joint attention*. We see this when your child points to something he wants or something he's interested in, then at you, then back at the object, and so forth. We want to see him combine talking, gestures, body language and eye contact to do this.

When a child combines all these together to show he's interested in something, that's a big win for language development! Joint attention is so important that if we don't see it, we need to evaluate further for potential problems in development.

Here are two things I want you to take away from this. First, I hope you appreciate it if you see progress in any of these aspects of language. Does your child give you a hug to comfort you when she senses you're sad? Don't take it for granted. Not only does it melt your heart, but it's also a great example of interactive communication.

Second, I want to emphasize that it's the methods described in this book that will help your toddler develop all these aspects of language. Learning apps, educational videos, flashcard drills, and worksheets will not build true interactive language.

The Difference between Speech and Language

Technically, speech is how we say sounds and words.

Language, on the other hand, is a system of communication. It's not limited to spoken language, but it includes written language (reading and writing) and other forms of communication such as sign language.

When we observe a child's language, we look at these components:[2]

1. Phonology: the sounds in a language, including how to put these sounds together.

2. Vocabulary or semantics: knowing the meaning of words and having a good inventory of words to use. Often, people notice only these first two aspects of language. But we need to build the other parts too.

3. Morphology: how the smallest units of language are used to form words and carry meaning. For example, in English, understanding that adding "s" makes a word plural is part of morphology.

4. Syntax: the rules of how words are arranged and combined into sentences. For example, from "Hop on Pop" by Dr. Seuss, "Mouse on house" is different from "house on mouse." (I love Dr. Seuss's books for building language skills.)

5. Pragmatics: the social aspects of language that affect how effectively a person will communicate. Using the proper intonation. Taking turns in conversation. Knowing you talk to another

[2] There's an excellent discussion of this by the American Speech-Language-Hearing Association (ASHA). Visit https://www.asha.org/practice-portal/clinical-topics/spoken-language-disorders/language-in-brief/.

child differently from how you would talk to an older adult, especially one who isn't familiar to you.

Often, we take this aspect of language for granted. But when kids don't learn this, they're often labeled as "naughty" or "disrespectful," when in reality, it may be a difficulty with understanding the pragmatics of language. That's why I emphasize the social aspect of language throughout this book.

This book focuses not just on speech, but on the entirety of language development. Sometimes I use the term "speech delay" when the more technically accurate term is "language delay." That's because most parents are more familiar with the term "speech delay."

Why Language Development is So Important during the Baby and Toddler Years

If you want an analogy of what can happen if we don't build the right foundation, think of the infamous traffic situation in Manila. Traffic can get so horrible that cars move at the speed of inches per hour. Flyovers, major roadworks, and even the most brilliant rules and schemes can't solve the problem. Wouldn't it have been better if the roads were planned and built the right way from the start?

The same thing goes for the brain. During the baby and toddler years, your child's brain develops rapidly, building foundations that will last a lifetime.

Decades ago, most people thought that when babies are born, they don't sense what's around them.

Because of this belief, many caregivers treated babies almost like inanimate objects. As a child growing up, I remember seeing nannies mechanically feed or bathe babies and change diapers without talking to or even looking at them. Babies were left in cribs most of the day, to the point that many babies' heads were flattened at the back.

Today, we know that even during the newborn period, there's more to babies than just eating, sleeping, and pooping. It's not true that your baby doesn't sense what's going on around her. On the contrary, her brain already takes in the stimuli.

Your baby's early experiences shape how she learns and grows. This goes both ways. She shapes her environment too! Even at birth, she already has their own personality that influences how others interact with her.

The best time to stimulate language and brain development is now, during the early years. Research shows the importance of the first one thousand days—from mom's pregnancy all the way until a child turns two. This is when it's easiest to make the greatest impact on your child's life.

The first few years of life are what scientists call the sensitive period for brain development. If a baby doesn't receive the right kind of stimulation during this time, it will be very difficult, if not impossible, to catch up later on.

For example, we see this in babies born with a cataract. If we don't detect it early, even if we remove it later on, they will still be blind in that eye.

The following are some of the sensitive periods in a child's life:[3]

---

[3] "Improving the Odds: Healthy Child Development," Focus on the Early Years: Neuroscience and Implications for Clinical Practice. https://www.beststart.org/resources/hlthy_chld_dev/pdf/HCD_complete.pdf.

Sensitive Period	Age
Vision	Birth to 2 years
Hearing	Birth to 2 years
Emotional regulation	Birth to 5 years
Language	Birth to 4 years

Can we still make an impact later on? Yes we can, but it will be harder. In the words of Frederick Douglass, "It is easier to build strong children than to repair broken men."

That's why if you have a baby or a toddler, you're in the perfect position to give him the right kind of stimulation, while his brain is forming.

So, if a child has any delay in development, we want to identify it and start intervention as early as possible. It's not true that we should "wait until he's four" or "wait until she goes to school." By that time, the sensitive period is over! There's more about this in the chapter, "What To Do If You're Worried Your Child Might Have Speech Delay."

The Two Kinds of Language Milestones

Language isn't only about what your child says. What she understands is just as important. That's why we've classified language milestones into two categories, receptive and expressive.

Receptive language is how well your child understands what he hears

The following are some of the significant receptive language milestones in the first three years of life:

- Turning when you call his name.
- Knowing the things he sees every day (like a ball, block, or spoon).
- Understanding parts of the body.
- Following one-step commands—For example, "Give me the ball."
- Following two-step commands—For example, "Pack up your toys and wash your hands."

As early as when your child is a baby, we want to be sure that she specifically turns towards voices, and not only to environmental sounds that aren't voices.

Often, hearing problems in babies and young kids get diagnosed late because they do turn toward sounds. ("The sound of the electric fan bothers him," or "She reacts when a car passes by.") But the frequencies for these sounds are not necessarily the same as the frequencies for speech sounds. So it's possible for a baby or child to hear environmental sounds like a car horn, a bell, or something dropping to the floor—but not be able to hear speech sounds well.

Many people are surprised to learn that a baby's response to his name is a very important milestone. If your baby doesn't turn to his name by 12 months, he needs to be evaluated. This is actually quite late already, as most babies respond to their names long before this age.

Parents often say, "He doesn't respond to his name because he's always so busy. He's focused on playing with his toy." This is a myth. Neurotypical toddlers—no matter how busy they are—should respond to their name. They may not immediately stop what they're doing, but you'll see them pause briefly or show some sign they heard you.

Another common scenario is that a baby responded to her name in earlier months, say, seven or nine months. But by twelve months, she doesn't respond to her name anymore. If you observe this, you should also get a check-up for your child's development. Anytime we see a loss of a skill, it's a sign that your child needs to be evaluated.

Expressive language is what your child says, and the sounds and words that she makes

Expressive language starts even before your baby says her first word. Here are the "pre-talking" skills that babies go through when learning to talk.

Cooing

As a newborn, your baby's verbal communication consists of crying. She will cry to let you know she is hungry, tired, or uncomfortable. In the second month, she will start to make sounds other than crying. At first, these sounds will consist mostly of vowels. This is called cooing.

Babbling

When your baby is five to six months old, she will start to babble, or make sounds that consist of both consonants and vowels. These are repeated syllables, like dadada, tatata, mamama.

Around this time, your baby will also blow "raspberries." And here we thought this was just something cute she does! But these adorable "raspberries" are a sign that she'll start babbling soon.

Jargoning

Sometime before your child turns one, what she says will start sounding like "real" language. But the words may not be very clear yet. Most parents describe this as, "She sounds like she's speaking in a foreign language!"

This is called jargoning. We call it "immature" jargoning if we can't understand any of the words, and "mature" jargoning if some of the words are clear.

Around your child's first birthday, get ready for an exciting time. He'll soon speak his first real word! From then on, your child's language skills will accelerate. By the time he turns two, he'll typically be able to use 50 words and be able to put two words together in a sentence.

Your child's vocabulary should include different kinds of words. Some will refer to people (mom, dad); everyday objects (ball, spoon); things she is interested in (animals or things she sees around her); and maybe a few adjectives and action words (cold, ouch, play, eat).

If your child's vocabulary consists entirely of one thing, such as names of vehicles only (car, truck, and maybe even makes and models of different cars and trucks), your child may also need an evaluation.

CHAPTER 2

IS MY CHILD'S LANGUAGE DEVELOPMENT ON TRACK? MILESTONES IN LANGUAGE DEVELOPMENT

> *"Childhood is not a race to see how quickly a child can read, write and count. It is a small window of time to learn and develop at the pace that is right for each individual child. Earlier is not better."*
>
> **—Magda Gerber**

I F A CHILD's development isn't on track, we want to know this as soon as possible so we don't miss out on the best time to help the child.

Many times, we see kids with language delay only when they're about to enroll in kindergarten or first grade (or even later). That's the only time anyone notices the delay. Sadly, this means they end up missing out on the best time to receive intervention for language delays.

However, I'd also like to warn you against the opposite extreme— what some parents call "milestone anxiety." I'm seeing this more often, and it causes a great deal of stress for both parents and kids.

Here are some examples of milestone anxiety.

- You scroll through your Instagram feed and see one-year-old babies attending online classes and learning the alphabet. You start to feel guilty, and you worry your baby might be behind.

- You see a mom posting to Facebook that her eighteen-month-old can name all the pictures on a set of flash cards. You can't even get your baby to name one. When you try to get her to sit and memorize flash cards, all she wants to do is grab them and chatter excitedly.

Adding to milestone anxiety is how people like to compare one child with another, especially in the family. This takes a toll not just on parents but on kids too. At that young age, they already feel that they're displeasing the adults in their lives, but they don't understand why or what it is they're doing wrong.

Do you go around comparing your weight with others? For example, do you post on Facebook and ask, "I'm 150 pounds. I want to know if this is okay. How much do you weigh and how are you doing?" Intuitively, we know that's not a good idea (not to mention a post like that may get called out as "weight shaming"!). There will always be people who weigh less or more than you. Most will be doing fine, and a few will have health problems which may or may not be related to weight.

Instead, you or your doctor will check what's the healthy weight for someone of your height. This isn't based on people's opinions, but on what research has shown to lower the risk for medical complications. This won't be just one number, but it will be a range. It's similar for child development.

Many moms who worry about their child's development may start comparing and asking around, "My two-year-old isn't talking yet. Is this okay? When did your child learn to talk?"

But if you want to know whether your child's development is on track, it's not a good idea to go around comparing with his cousins, other kids in a toddler class, or the kids of other moms in a Facebook group. The best way is to use objective standards. Although child development is not as clear cut as your weight or a blood test result, there are objective "evidence-informed" standards.[4]

Comparing with other kids will either cause you a lot of stress or make you falsely complacent. You'll surely hear stories of other kids who seem so much more advanced, and you'll worry. Or you'll hear stories like, "Don't worry, my child didn't talk until he was four!"—and you'll miss out on the best time to help your child.

Child development is not a contest. Each child has her own unique strengths and challenges, and her own timeline. There are so many individual variations in how kids develop.

The best way to know whether your child's development is on track is to go through developmental surveillance and screening, which I'll describe in chapter 10 of this book. Pediatricians do this during regular check-ups, or what we call "well-child visits."

---

[4] Zubler, et al. 2022. "Evidence-informed milestones for developmental surveillance tools." *Pediatrics*.

I'm Confused. Why Do I Sometimes See Different Ages for The Same Milestone?

For each milestone, there are actually three ages that research studies track.

The first is what we call the *initial* age. This is generally the earliest age that we expect a child to be able to perform a skill. The age where, based on research, the first few children start to show that ability.

We don't want to push a child to perform a milestone long before the initial age. This will just be a source of frustration! The brain architecture just isn't there yet. Getting a child to perform a skill without this necessary brain architecture is like trying to add wallpaper to a house when the foundation isn't even done.

The second is what we call the *median* age. This is the age when 50 percent of kids can perform a skill. Until 2021, most charts on developmental milestones gave this age. For example, a developmental milestone chart will say that your child says his first word around the time of the first birthday. It does not mean your child will perform this skill at exactly that age. What this means is that roughly 50 percent of kids will actually do this a little earlier, while 50 percent will do this a little later. But based on the research studies, most kids will cluster around this age.

The third is what we call the *limit* age. If your child hasn't achieved a milestone by the limit age, intervention will be needed.

In 2022, the Center for Disease and Communication (CDC) and the American Academy of Pediatrics (AAP) released a new set of milestones that are now based on when 75 percent of kids can perform a skill. This means that in the new checklists, some skills were moved to later ages. Instead of the median ages from the older charts, the ages given are now limit ages.[4]

To clearly illustrate the concepts of initial, median, and limit ages, I'd like to use the example of walking. The initial age for walking independently, without holding on to anything, is at nine months. That's because the "speed boost" in the pathways needed for walking happens at around this time. So you can spend all day giving "walking lessons" to your five- or six-month-old, but this won't get her walking on her own by seven months.

The median age for walking is twelve months. By this age, roughly half of all babies will have taken their first independent steps. Your child may start walking a little before, or a little after twelve months.

The limit age for walking is eighteen months. If your child isn't walking independently by eighteen months, an evaluation and intervention will be needed.

However, if your doctor feels that your child needs help, we don't want to wait until the limit age to see whether or not your child will achieve the milestone. We start helping your child way before this age.

I use the updated 2022 CDC milestones in this chapter because this set of milestones emphasizes the interactive aspect of communication. For example, a new milestone is that at six months, your baby will take turns making sounds with you. This important skill—taking turns—wasn't in the old set of milestones.

Not all professionals in the child development field agree with the 2022 revision. Some feel these milestones are too late.[5]

So in part III of this book, I included the language milestones by the American Speech-Language-Hearing Association, which are closer

---

[5] https://leader.pubs.asha.org/do/10.1044/2022-0314-cdc-milestones-update/full/.

to the median ages. Don't be confused if the ages are somewhat different from what's in this chapter.

Here are two takeaways from this. First, if your child isn't meeting any of the expected skills mentioned in this chapter, follow the steps in chapter ten. No more wondering about whether or not you're overreacting.

This applies even for babies and very young kids. Even if it's a two-month-old who doesn't make sounds other than crying, or a four-month-old who doesn't make sounds back when you talk to her—it's not too early to seek consultation.

Second, pediatricians don't rely only on milestone checklists for early detection of developmental delays. The entire process includes interviewing you, observing your child, and doing screening tests. I also explain this in chapter ten.

If a baby or child has risk factors, we don't need to wait and see when they will reach developmental milestones. Doctors can recommend intervention even as early as during the newborn period. We do this, for example, for babies who are born premature, or patients with genetic conditions such as Down syndrome.

Receptive Language Milestones[6]

Here are the major milestones in how kids understand what they hear.

Age	Milestone
2 months	Reacts to loud sounds
4 months	Turns head towards the sound of your voice
12 months	Understands no
15 months	Looks at a familiar object when you name it Follows directions when given with both a gesture and words. For example, when you say, "Give me the ball" and you point to the ball, he hands it over.
18 months	Follows one-step commands without any gestures.
2 years	Points to things in a book when you ask, "Where is the bear?" Points to at least two body parts when you ask him to show you
2 ½ years	Follows two-step instructions such as, "Put the toy down and close the door." Shows that she knows at least one color, like pointing to a red crayon when you ask, "Which is red?"

Expressive Language Milestones

Age	Milestone
2 months	Makes sounds other than crying
4 months	Makes sounds like "oooh" and "aaah" (cooing) Makes sounds back when you talk to her
6 months	Takes turns making sounds with you Blows raspberries (sticks tongue out and blows) Makes squealing noises
9 months	Makes different sounds like "mamamama" and "bababab"
12 months	Waves bye bye Calls a parent "mama," "dada," or another special name
15 months	Tries to say 1-2 words besides "mama" or "dada" Points to ask for something or to get help
2 years	Says at least two words together, such as "more milk" Uses more gestures than just waving or pointing, such as blowing a kiss or nodding yes
2 ½ years	Says about 50 words Says two or more words, one of which is an action word (ex. "Doggie run") Uses words such as "I," "we," or "me" Names things in a book when you point and ask, "What's this?"

3 years	Has conversations with you, with at least two back-and-forth exchanges
	Asks who, what, where and why questions
	Says what action is happening in a picture or a book, such as "running" or "playing"
	Says first name when asked
	Talks well enough for other people to understand him most of the time

NOTES:

1. Kids should be able to meet *all* the milestones for their age. If they miss even *one*, they'll need further evaluation. For example, a 2 1/2-year-old can say about 50 words and name things in a book when you point to them. However, if he doesn't have two-word sentences or doesn't use pronouns, investigate further.

2. At three years of age, kids talk well enough for other people to understand them most of the time. Parents often ask, "When should my child be able to speak clearly?" We had a rule of thumb for this: the child's age divided by four is the percent of the child's speech that should be understandable. So:

At the age of...	Other people should be able to understand at least...
1 year	¼ or 25%
2 years	2/4 or 50%
3 years	¾ or 75%
4 years	The child should be speaking clearly

We also need to watch out for the loss of milestones at any age. Here are some examples:

- Your child used to say a few words, and then stops talking.
- Your child used to be able to look at you, call you "mama," and use gestures, but he doesn't do these anymore.

If your child has lost a skill, tell your pediatrician about it.

The Goal of Language Development During the Toddler Years

A child should be fully conversational—able to ask and answer questions in an interactive conversation—by age three. Here's an example of a conversation.

Mommy: "Hey, what are you doing? That looks interesting!"
Child: "I'm building a tower!"

> A child should be fully conversational by age three.

This is the goal of language development during the toddler years. Don't worry about rote memorization of the alphabet, numbers, or other academic concepts. Comprehension and interactive communication are more important.

A perfect example of rote memory without comprehension is when a child can recite the numbers one through twenty, or even through fifty. However, when we show him two blocks and ask, "How many?" he can't say, "Two!" It's far more important for a child to understand the concept of "two" rather than recite numbers without knowing what they mean.

That's why when I say "ask and answer questions in conversation," I don't mean doing drills. These might be useful at an older age, but not during the toddler years.

This is not the kind of conversation I'm talking about:

Mommy: "What's this?" (Shows a flash card.)

Child: "Apple."

On the other hand, this is a better conversation, even if all baby did was babble:

Mommy (while looking at baby): "Wow, look at this shiny red apple. Apples are healthy and yummy. Let's eat this apple together!"

Baby babbles. (While looking at mommy and smiling.)

Mommy: "Oh, you like it, don't you?"

This book comes with an online resource library that includes a PDF guide on developmental milestones. Get it now at toddlertalkingbook.com.

Common Questions about Developmental Milestones

When you say, for example, a two-and-a-half-year-old should have fifty words, what counts as a word?

A word is anything that a child uses meaningfully and consistently in order to communicate.

In the clinic, each test we use may have its own system for counting words. For example, some tests would count mommy, daddy, grandma, grandpa as four words. Others will count all people's names as just one word. Some tests will accept word approximations (such as "baw" for "ball"), while others don't.

Despite these differences in how to count words, once we've finished the scoring and interpretation, the tests are still consistent with each other in helping us evaluate whether a child's development is on track.

So don't obsess over counting your child's words. There's no need to agonize over whether that cute thing she said counts as a word. It's interactive communication that's important. For example, if your child can talk about what happened (ex. "milk spill"), that's great! I'd worry more about a child who, for example, can name a flash card for milk, but can't say "milk" when she wants some.

The internet also has plenty of lists. "100 words your child needs to know by age two." These lists are not research-validated. There's nothing magical about these words. So as long as your child knows a variety of words, it doesn't have to be these words in particular! Stop worrying about these word lists. Focus on interacting with your child instead.

When we assess a child's language development, we consider words in all the languages that a family uses. If your child uses one language to refer to some things and another language for others, you can count all of them.

Do kids need to learn the developmental milestones in order?

In general, we expect kids to develop these milestones in order. For example, a child should be able to say "mama" and "papa" before learning to count or memorize nursery rhymes.

Some kids have what we call "splinter skills". This means a child has a skill for a more advanced age group, but hasn't achieved the milestones for an earlier age. One example is a two-year-old who has memorized the names of the dinosaurs and can count to fifty, but can't say "mama" and "papa."

Kids who don't meet the milestones for their own age still need help with their development, even if they have some "advanced" skills. I want to emphasize this, because this is one reason why many kids don't get the help they need. The splinter skills mask the child's speech delay.

Common Myths About Language Development

Myth: It's normal for boys to have speech delay

I hear this often. If a boy isn't talking yet at age two, people say, "Oh don't worry. There's no need to get an evaluation. That's because he's a boy! Boys really talk late." Research does show that around twice as many boys are diagnosed with speech delay compared with girls.

However, whether your child is a boy or a girl, he or she will still follow the same set of milestones. Unlike weight or height, for example, there's no separate set of milestones for boys and girls.

If you're worried about your son's language development, don't wait it out just because he's a boy. Regardless of gender, you'll want to intervene early on.

Myth: "Babying" causes language delays

This is another common myth. "Oh, of course she doesn't talk. That's because we baby her and give her everything she wants!"

Kids *should* talk. Even if they're given "everything they want." (And come on, is it even possible to give toddlers "everything they want"?

Including never going to sleep, painting your sofa green, and going inside the washing machine?)

Kids talk not just about what they want, but also about what they're interested in. Did your child point to your neighbor's parrot and chatter animatedly? Or launch into a tale about the sandwich she had for breakfast (and leave you wondering what's so exciting about it)? These are perfect examples of the kind of communication we want to see.

Sometimes, if a child has speech delay, some therapists may recommend not immediately giving a child something unless he says the correct name. This doesn't apply to everyone though, and it should be used only on a case-to-case basis. It does *not* mean that giving the child what he wants caused the speech delay.

Myth: Speaking more than one language at home causes delay

"It's okay that my child isn't talking yet. It's because we speak two languages at home."

We don't use a separate set of standards for kids from bilingual or multilingual homes. Even if your family speaks different languages, a neurotypical child will be able to process them. So when talking with your child, go ahead and use all the languages your family speaks.

During the baby and toddler years, your child can learn to use a language like a native speaker if other people interact with him in that language. By this, I mean actual, everyday-life conversations with a human being. The baby and toddler years are not the time for formal language lessons or language learning apps or videos.

If your child already has speech delay, his doctor or therapist may advise sticking to one language until he's built up enough communication skills in that language. But this does not mean that the multiple languages caused the delay.

When Do Kids Need to Learn Written Language?

Many parents worry about when their kids should learn to read and write. One of the biggest sources of stress for toddler parents is, "My three-year-old doesn't know the alphabet!" Many parents are told, "Your child should read CVC (consonant-vowel-consonant) words at age three."

According to the American Academy of Pediatrics, "*Some* children learn to read at four to five years of age. *Most* children learn by six to seven years."[7] In the 2022 developmental milestones, "names some letters when you point to them" is listed at five years of age.

Here are some milestones for reading.[8]

A three-year-old:

- recognizes a book by its cover
- pretends to read books
- understands that books are handled in certain ways
- may pay attention to print such as letters and numbers

[7] "Helping Your Child Learn to Read." https://www.healthychildren.org/English/ages-stages/preschool/Pages/Helping-Your-Child-Learn-to-Read.aspx.
[8] "A Child Becomes a Reader: Proven Ideas from Research." National Institute of Literacy. https://lincs.ed.gov/publications/pdf/reading_pre.pdf.

By the time they are five, we expect them to:

- recognize print on signs, boxes, and many other places
- know that each letter of the alphabet has a name
- name most (*not all*) letters of the alphabet

That's it! We don't expect them to sight read, recognize CVC words, write entire words, or any of the other crazy things that many people want these young kids to do. There's no advantage to learning to decode words at, say, age three compared to age six.

Also, I can't stress this enough—before learning written language, kids need to develop listening comprehension and interactive communication.

The most important thing to develop at this age is a love for learning. This is exactly what we'll destroy if we force our kids to learn things before they're ready. Then, when the time comes that they actually do need to learn how to read, it will be harder for them.

That's why I'm bothered when I see toddlers (and their moms!) in tears, battling over worksheets and reading lessons. I feel bad for the moms who feel shamed into doing all of this.

The toddler stage is challenging enough. Don't make your child's "terrible two's" or "threenager phase" harder for your child and for yourself with these unrealistic expectations.

If you're worried about your child's learning and development, instead of stressing about it or buying all the "learn to read" apps advertised on your Facebook feed, speak with your pediatrician or a developmental pediatrician.

3 Myths About Learning to Read

Myth: An advertisement for a "reading program" claims, "This program will teach your child to read by age two!" or "Teach your child to read in 30 days." A video shows a toddler "reading" letters of the alphabet or sight words.

Truth: Learning the alphabet or recognizing sight words are not the same as knowing how to read. "Reading" is made up of a number of different skills. These include appreciating sounds and rhymes, as well as actually *understanding* what the text says. This means that for a child to truly read, she must already have good language comprehension skills.

Sometimes I hear, "My child learned to read even before he can talk." This may be a sign of a condition known as hyperlexia. Children with hyperlexia would need to be evaluated by a developmental and behavioral pediatrician. A review of multiple researches showed that 84 percent of kids with hyperlexia are in the autism spectrum.[9]

Myth: My child can recite the alphabet and recognize words. So even if he can't talk, I'm sure he doesn't have language delay.

Truth: A child who recognizes printed letters and words can still have language delay.

Unfortunately, this is a common myth. It's a reason why some kids miss out on early intervention. Because the child has memorized the alphabet, and often can also count, recite nursery rhymes, and even name dinosaurs, countries, or a number of other things, no one realizes the child actually has language delays.

---

[9] Ostrolenk, et al. 2017. "Hyperlexia: Systematic review, neurocognitive modelling, and outcome." *Neuroscience and Biobehavioral Reviews.*

If a child has memorized the alphabet or can say many words, but cannot make simple requests or tell us (even in simple ways) about something that happened, the child can have speech delay.

Myth: We need to teach kids to read as early as possible. Kids will be more successful if we push reading during the toddler years.

Truth: Early reading isn't associated with better or more successful outcomes. [10]

It can be quite impressive to see a video of a toddler "reading" words out loud. Many moms see these videos and think, "I'm such a bad mom. I haven't started reading lessons with my two-year-old!" If that's you, stop feeling guilty right now. You have scientific research on your side.[11]

When your child grows up and has her first job interview, no employer will ask, "When did you learn to read? Were you reciting the alphabet at age three?" But she will need to express herself accurately and fluently. She'll need to understand the interviewer's nonverbal signals, and also project body language that shows she's the best person for the job.

I hope more parents realize this. It's sad to see moms get stressed and guilty if their three-year-old kids haven't memorized the alphabet or learned to read. Preschool teachers also tell me they hear

---

[10] Leahy and Fitzpatrick. 2017. "Early Readers and Academic Success." *Journal of Educational and Developmental Psychology.* Kern and Friedman. 2009. "Early educational milestones as predictors of lifelong academic achievement, midlife adjustment, and longevity." *Journal of Applied Developmental Psychology.*

[11] In fact, the large and long-term study on gifted children done by Kern and Friedman (2009) showed, "Early reading was associated with early educational success, but was also associated with worse long-term outcomes including less overall educational attainment, worse teenage and adult adjustment, and increased alcohol use." This is not to alarm parents whose kids truly enjoy reading for pleasure early on. Rather, what we can take away from this is that there's no correlation between early reading and long-term success.

complaints like, "Her cousin's school makes the kids memorize the alphabet. Why aren't you?"

The flip side of the coin is also true. If a child has memorized the alphabet but doesn't have eye contact or conversational speech, often people don't realize the child needs intervention.

I understand we're all worried about our kids' future and we want to give our kids all the advantages they can get.

However, when we make kids learn to read before they're ready, they don't learn it well. From kindergarten to first grade and onwards, everyone assumes that reading should've already been taught in the previous level.

But if we wait for developmental readiness, kids will be able to truly understand, absorb and enjoy what they're learning. THIS is what will give them the advantage.[12] Not pushing reading lessons to earlier ages.

---

[12] Check out our article and podcast episodes on the importance of waiting for readiness, and helping kids learn to read. https://discerningparenting.com/helping-your-child-learn-to-read/

PART II

Three Powerful Strategies
to Help Your
Toddler Learn to Talk

CHAPTER 3

TALK WITH YOUR CHILD

> *"Tell me and I forget, teach me and I may remember,*
> *involve me and I learn."*
>
> **—Xun Kuang, Chinese Confucian philosopher**

IF WE WANT OUR kids to learn to talk, we need to talk with them in a way that actually *involves* them in our conversations and daily lives.

With all the distractions of life today, sometimes we forget about this. Raise your hand if you've ever observed this at a restaurant. An entire family is eating together, but everyone is glued to their own devices. No one's talking with each other.

It can happen at home, at a family gathering, or even on vacation at a lovely beach. If we're not mindful, we can end up spending more quality time with our phones than our loved ones.

Unfortunately, if we don't talk with our babies and toddlers, their language development suffers.

A couple of decades ago, a study recruited 42 families from different income levels who had babies 7-9 months old. As these babies were learning to talk, the researchers recorded and observed what went on in their homes.[13]

The results? Babies and toddlers from professional families heard many more spoken words and experienced more positive interactions compared with kids from low-income families. By age three, they already had wider vocabularies.

By computing the difference in words these kids heard and multiplying by the waking hours, the researchers estimated that by the time these kids reached the age of three, those from wealthier families heard thirty million more words compared with kids from the low income families. This is famously known as the "30-million-word gap."

Fast forward to 2018, when another research showed exactly what happens in our kids' brains when we talk with them. This study found that kids who had more conversational turns with adults also had more activation in the parts of their brains that produce speech (called the Broca's area).[14]

The takeaway from this is that it's not about income level, but about whether or not you actually have conversations with your child. Simply *talking* with your child makes a difference in his brain—a difference we can actually see in brain studies.

So, talk with your child. Then pause, and let your child respond. These back-and-forth conversations will boost your child's brain development.

---

[13] Hart and Risley. 2003. "The Early Catastrophe: The 30 Million Word Gap by Age 3." *American Educator*.
[14] Romeo et al. 2018. "Beyond the 30 Million Word Gap: Children's Conversational Exposure is Associated with Language-Related Brain Function." *Psychological Science*.

What to Talk about—It's as Easy as PQRST

"But what do I talk about? What do I say?"

If your child is already asking questions nonstop (and I can tell you—it really is *nonstop*!), this may not be a problem for you. But many parents of babies and young kids who aren't talking yet often feel at a loss about how to have a conversation.

The simple answer is—talk about anything and everything! What's happening. What you're doing. What's going on in your mind.

A leaf fell to the ground. You're not sure which shoes to wear. You want to pick your nose. Nothing is too insignificant to be a conversation topic.

To make it easier, remember PQRST.

POINT to things around you and tell your child about them.

Label and talk about the things you see and experience. Focus on conversation, not academic knowledge or rote repetition.

Your child learns not just from what you say, but from the entire experience of communicating with you. Watching how your mouth and lips move. Seeing your facial expressions. Hearing your excited voice when you describe something you like. Getting a hug while you speak comforting words.

Here are examples of things you can say:

"Look at the beautiful clouds in the sky! You can see them moving."

"I'm going to make sandwiches for us. See how I get the bread and put butter on it?"

"Look at my shoes! They're a nice blue color. They have laces, see? The laces are tied in a ribbon."

Engage as many senses as possible. "Do you want to touch this glass of water? It's cold." "What does it sound like when the door creaks open?" Or "I smell something baking in the oven. What do you think it is?" We learn and remember things better when they're multisensory experiences.

Your child's different senses come together when learning language. Seeing the actual thing, whether it's a rose, a bulldozer, or a basketball that another kid is tossing around. Touching the leaves of trees and feeling the wind blowing gently. Smelling flowers or freshly cut grass. Tasting a bowl of soup. Hearing a cat meow or a motorcycle pass by. Being carried and rocked. Jumping up and down. Even recognizing the need to pee.

That's why I discourage using flash cards for babies and young toddlers. These don't provide the context and multisensory experiences that your child needs when learning to talk. If you really want, you may get *one* set of flashcards, maybe as your child nears the age of three. But they're no substitute for allowing your toddler to explore the environment safely.

If you want to introduce academic knowledge, it's best to wait until your child is already talking. Some examples are, "Point to things that start with the B sound." or "How many slices of apple would you like?" Be careful, though, that you do this a relaxed manner, and not like a classroom drill.

Ask QUESTIONS, even if your child can't verbally answer yet

Even before your baby learns to talk, start asking questions. "Oh, is that a doggie I hear?" "I smell something yummy. I wonder what that is?" "Would you like apple juice or orange juice?" While your child is playing, ask questions like, "What's teddy doing?" This builds language, critical thinking, and creativity.

Tips on Asking Questions

Make sure it really is a question.

Unless it's really okay with you if your child doesn't brush his teeth, don't ask, "Would you like to brush your teeth?" Instead, ask, "Do you want to use your Minions toothbrush or your Batman toothbrush?"

Use age-appropriate questions.

Questions are a fun way to help your child improve vocabulary, learn concepts, and interact with you. Here are some examples of questions you can ask at different ages.

Baby	Oh, your diaper is wet, isn't it?
	Would you like to try holding the green spoon or the blue one?
	Do you like to try the banana or the avocado?
	What do we have here? Oh, isn't this a nice and shiny rattle?
1 year	Where's the cat?
	Do you want to play with the big, red ball?
	Which toy do you want to bring to the bath?
	Which book do you want to read?

2 years	Which one is bigger?
	How many slices of bread do you want?
	Can you point to all the red things you see?
	How do you think your sister is feeling right now?
	What can we do to help you next time, so you don't hit your playmate?

Wait for the answer, listen and respond. I have to remind myself to do this too! How often do we ask our kids questions then we don't really let them answer? So, after asking - stop, look and listen. Your child may "answer" with gestures, pointing, babbling, or words.

As your child nears three years of age, she'll constantly ask you a ton of questions. And I do mean *a ton!* Tired of answering a hundred questions a day? Give yourself a break by saying, "That's a great question! What do you think?"

RESPOND to what your child says or does

Out of ideas? Take a cue from your child. Even if all we do is observe our kids, we'll never run out of things to say! When your baby smiles or makes a gesture, notice it. If your child says something, look at him. Smile or say something in return. You can also describe what your child does.

When your child says something that is not clear, try repeating it more clearly. "Expound" on what he says by adding words or turning what he says into sentences.

For example, your baby says, "tatatata" while playing with her trucks. Say, "Oh, you want to play with the dump truck? You're dumping out all the blocks." Then pause and smile encouragingly as she babbles some more.

Use SONGS and rhymes

Action songs and rhymes are great ways to learn language. They're a fun, easy, no-prep activity, and a great way to connect with young kids.

Rhymes may seem simple, but they actually set the stage for your child to understand the basic units of sounds (called "phonemes"). And phoneme awareness is one of the requirements before a child can really learn to read. That's why a child who can't appreciate rhymes by age 5 may be at risk for reading disorders.

Here are some popular songs and what your child can learn from them. I point these out to help you appreciate that even some-thing simple can have lessons included. But I certainly don't want you to think that everything you sing with your child needs to have a lesson!

- "The Wheels on the Bus"—adjectives, opposites, and sounds
- "If You're Happy and You Know It"—emotions and actions
- "Head, Shoulders, Knees, and Toes" or "Hokey Pokey"— body parts
- "The Ants Go Marching"—numbers and body awareness
- "Hey Diddle Diddle"—sounds and rhyming

"Hickory Dickory Dock," "Twinkle Twinkle Little Star," and "Incy Wincy Spider" are great for this too.

For basic numeracy skills, one of my favorite songs is "One Potato, Two Potato." As a toddler, my child loved this song and sang it when eating . . . well, . . . potatoes. And he's tried substituting "potato" for whatever he's eating at the moment.

Almost all action songs help with body awareness if you move along as you sing. "I'm a Little Teapot," "The Noble Duke of York"—and I'm sure you have your favorites too.

TELL your child about what's happening and TEACH even about the simple things

Talk with your child as you go about your daily activities. You can do this anytime throughout the day. Meal time, bath time, diaper changing time, clean-up-the-mess time – these are all great opportunities for conversations.

Comment about what's around you. What you're doing, thinking, or feeling. Here are some examples:

- "Oh! There's a bee outside. Do you see it? Can you point to it? Can you hear it buzz? We have to be careful. Bees can sting!"

- Busy doing the dishes? You can still connect with your child. "Oh look! I'm using the sponge to wash the plate."

- "I'm feeling a bit tired after all that playing. I'm thirsty too. I'll have a drink and sit down and rest for a while. Would you like some water too?"

We may feel that "nothing's happening," or there's nothing really worth talking about. But that's not true. *Everything* is interesting for your baby or toddler. If you've ever had your toddler throw a tantrum because she wanted to grab the rag you're using to wipe the table, you know what I mean.

Be elaborate! When you're simply conversing with your child, don't worry about whether you're using words that he already understands. Don't be afraid to use big words.

Pause and let your child respond too. Even if your child says nothing, keep at it. You'll see how your baby or toddler will look at you and focus on your face. She'll just love hearing your voice.

"Talk-alongs" and "think-alouds" are a busy parent's best tools for building language skills. If you really need to do something anyway, you might as well talk about it and verbalize what you're thinking.

For example, if you're getting your child dressed, you can say, "I wonder which shirt you should wear today? It's a bit warm so I think you can wear a thinner shirt. What do you think? Do you want to wear your blue dinosaur shirt, or your yellow Spider-man shirt?"

> "Talk-alongs" and "think-alouds" are a busy parent's best tools for building language skills.

I also try do this while working from home. For example, if I'm planning my week, I turn it into a conversation with my child as I write out my task lists. This is a great way to get some work done while still engaging with your child. Your work may not get done as quickly, but if you can afford spending the extra time, it's definitely worth it.

Why is it important to use language in everyday situations? This is an example of how we work with your child's brain, not against it.

The part of our brains responsible for creating long-term memory and learning is called the hippocampus. The hippocampus gets activated and remembers things better when something is necessary for our survival.

That's why it's such a struggle to get kids to memorize flash cards and the alphabet! Our brains aren't wired that way. For example, compare these two situations.

Situation 1:
A child is attending an online class. The teacher flashes a photo of an apple on the screen and says, "A is for apple."

Situation 2:
It's snack time. There's an apple and an orange on the table. Mom says, "It's snack time. I'm feeling hungry. You must be hungry too! Which one do you like, the apple or the orange?" The child touches both of them and selects the apple. Mom and child eat the apple together. Mom says, "This apple is red, juicy and sweet. It's good for you too!"

In which situation do you think the child will be more likely to learn vocabulary?

In the first situation, the child might learn to recite by rote, "A is for apple." But it doesn't build conversation skills. It's a constant struggle to keep the information because it's not related to everyday life. That's why I see so many parents saying, "My child has been attending classes for some time, but doesn't know the alphabet yet!" Or, "We fight each time I try to get my child to sit and answer worksheets/learn from flashcards."

In the second situation, before long, the child learns to use words meaningfully. She learns the meaning of words, and when and how to use it. Soon she'll be saying, "I'm hungry. I'd like an apple please!"

When the child has understood this, *and* when the time is right, it will be much easier to teach "A is for apple" because she truly understands the concepts behind it.

Tips for Talking With Your Child

Use parentese when talking with babies

Research shows that using parentese helps babies eighteen months and below to learn language.[15] That's why when talking with babies, most people instinctively switch to parentese.

Here are the characteristics of parentese:

- higher pitch
- exaggerated changes in intonation
- stretched out sounds
- repetition
- shorter and simpler sentences

Speaking in parentese means still using the correct sentence structure and pronunciation. We definitely shouldn't worry

---

[15] Ramirez et al. 2020. "Parent Coaching Increases Conversational Turns and Advances Infant Language Development." *Proceedings of the National Academy of Sciences.*

about using perfect grammar and pronunciation, but don't deliberately make errors either. It won't be helpful to say, "We is wabby wabby dawgee." Better to simply say, "We love the doggy!" while exaggerating the sounds and using an animated voice.

Use a variety of words

Kids need to learn the different kinds of words that we use. They need to hear them in action and in everyday situations. This is another reason why we can't rely on flash cards or all those toddler word lists that are so popular on the internet.

When you talk with your child, go ahead and use:

- Nouns of different categories (food, animals, people, etc.)
- Pronouns
- Verbs
- Adjectives
- Adverbs
- Prepositions
- Conjunctions (connecting words like and, or, but)
- Numbers and quantifiers (some, many)
- Filler words such as "oh" and even "uhhmm"—You'd be surprised that it's important for your child to hear words like these too.[16]

---

[16] Kidd, et al. 2011. "Toddlers use speech dysfluencies to predict speakers' referential intentions." *Developmental Science.*

Include plenty of gestures and actions

When talking with your child, look at her so that she sees your gestures and facial expression. The younger the child, the more you'll need to add gestures and actions.[17]

Sometimes we're so distracted when we talk with others that we don't even look at them anymore. But eye contact and the nonverbal part of communication are vital. So let's make it a point to really look at our kids when we talk with them.

Elaborate on what your child says

This is a great way to help your child learn language, because they get immediate feedback on their attempts to communicate.

Here are some examples of how to do this:

- Your child says, "ball" or something that sounds like it. Get a ball or point to one, and say, "Yes, this is a big, red ball! I bet we'll have fun playing with this ball."
- Your child says, "Milk!" (or however she says milk, like, "mimimi") You say, "Yes, you'd like to drink this glass of milk! This is yummy right?" Point to the glass of milk. "Would you like me to give you this glass of milk, or would you like to get the milk yourself?"

Here's what these examples have in common.

- What you say is related to what your child says, and it's also related to the situation.

---

[17] Masks can interfere with how young kids see our facial expressions and other nonverbal cues. Check out this excellent article by the American Speech-Language-Hearing Association on "Communicating Effectively While Wearing Masks." https://www.asha.org/public/communicating-effectively-while-wearing-masks-and-physical-distancing/.

- You're using what your child says as the starting point for a conversation.
- You repeatedly use real words that sound like what your child says.
- You combine your words with gestures and eye contact.

If you do this, you'll reinforce your child's first words and show her how to communicate. Don't overthink it! Just respond in a way that feels natural to you.

Describing something vs. giving commands

In this chapter, I encouraged you to be as elaborate as possible when talking with your child. It's different, however, with commands. When you narrate or describe something, be as elaborate as possible. But when you give a command, keep it clear and short.

Example of how you can be elaborate with a description:

"Oh look at that doggie! Isn't that a big, brown doggie? Look at how it's wagging its tail. Doesn't it look interested in those flowers? Oh it's on a leash and its owner is walking the dog. I wonder where they're going."

But with a command, be direct, clear and specific.

"It's time to pack away your toys. Would you like to put them in the red box or green box?" Or better yet, turn it into a game. "I'll race you! Let's see who can pack away more toys."

If you want to explain, do it as part of a conversation. As you're packing away, you can ask, "Why is it important to pack away your toys?" Pause and let your child respond. If your child says something that sounds like, "More play!" you can say, "Yes! So we don't lose your toys and we can have more fun playing!"

This is not the time to launch into a lecture about how your child never packs away toys, and you spend so much time looking for lost toys, and doesn't he know how expensive these toys are? And how he'll need to take care of his things and be responsible, and if he doesn't pack away,

> It's not about the words you say, but the relationship you build. The learning will happen.

later on he will ask you where his dinosaur toy is and you won't know because he didn't pack it away properly.

For more on this, check out my book, The Discerning Parent's Guide to Toddler Behavior: From Power Struggles to Connection.

Involve kids in family conversations

Young kids love to be part of what's going on around them. When adults or others in the family are talking, it's tempting to say, "Keep quiet. You're not a part of this." Or to laugh indulgently, then ignore them.

Remember, at this age, our kids' brains are forming connections between brain cells. If, from an early age, it's repeatedly embedded into those connections that "I'm not wanted in family conversations," don't be surprised when, as a teenager, your child will give nothing more than a grunt when you ask how his day went.

Making kids a part of family conversations from an early age does wonders for their development. It will:

- Build language and social skills.
- Raise their self-esteem. It teaches them that, in the words of *Positive Discipline* author Jane Nelsen, "I contribute in meaningful ways and am genuinely needed."
- Help make family relationships stronger.

At the start, what your toddler tries to contribute to the conversation may not make sense to you or other adults. But if you encourage his attempts to communicate, he'll gradually learn the skills for talking in a group.

Here are some examples:

Situation: Your toddler gives grandma a cupcake and says a lot of words that grandma doesn't understand.

Try this: "Want to share your cupcake with grandma? That's great! I think grandma appreciates it."

Situation: Mommy and daddy are talking, and your overexcited child interrupts with a story about the dog he saw that morning.

Try this: "Did what we say remind you of the dog? We'll let daddy finish what he's saying, then tell us your story."

If you're talking about something with another adult and your toddler is present, include your toddler in the conversation. If you really don't want your toddler to interrupt, it may be better to just have the conversation while someone else is taking care of your child.

You'll be surprised at how much toddlers can understand and remember. I can't count the number of times my child suddenly says something. When I ask where he heard it, he recounts a conversation he overheard days ago that I'd almost forgotten about!

Make it fun!

Above all, have fun. Don't stress about whether you're doing it right. Just talk with your child naturally as part of your daily routine. Focus on creating a connection with your child and enjoying the experience. It's not about the words you say, but the relationship you build. The learning will happen.

Take Action Today

Choose one part of your routine where you can include language stimulation. An easy win is to include this during meal times. Then add to another part of your routine, and so on.

If you're feeling overwhelmed and you just can't fit in yet another thing in your schedule, choose one task that you can eliminate. An example is preparing materials for complicated arts and crafts activities. Simpler activities will help develop these skills too, as you'll see in the next chapter.

CHAPTER 4

PLAY WITH YOUR CHILD

> *Imagine if pediatricians could write a prescription to help patients during the first two years of well-child visits that would boost social-emotional, cognitive, language and self-regulation skills. Research shows they can, and the "prescription" to write is simple: "Play with your child every day."*
>
> **—American Academy of Pediatrics**
>
> *Play is the highest form of research.*
>
> **—Albert Einstein**

WHEN YOU WERE a child, did anyone ever tell you, "Stop it! You're just playing!"

Many parents ask, "How can my toddler be more productive? He's just playing!" They feel compelled to fill kids' schedules with activities to teach, entertain, and keep them busy.

But play is how babies and young kids learn. At these ages, play *is* the most productive thing they can do. Play is a child's work!

How do we use play to build language skills? Allow child-led free play. Don't insist that your toddler sits at a table to play. Movement and exploration are vital to young kids' brain development.

Get down on the floor so you're at eye level with your child. Then follow your child's lead. As you do this, plenty of opportunities for language learning will naturally come up. This is a great time to do the PQRST Method from the previous chapter.

- **Point** to the toys and tell your child about them.
- Ask **questions**. "What are you doing?"
- **Respond** to what your child says. She'll surely bring her toys to you and try to talk with you about them.
- Use **songs** and rhymes. These are part of play too.
- **Tell** your child what's happening. When your child is doing something, you can expound on he's doing. "Wow, you're having your stuffed animals hug each other. That's a great way to show caring."

When we do developmental assessments, we spend a good part of it observing how kids play. Ideally, we want to see them play in different, age-appropriate ways. Some kids get stuck with only one way of playing. Others are great when they have step-by-step guides to follow, but don't know what to do when it comes to free play.

Unfortunately, parents get a lot of wrong advice about play. If you search the internet for "activities for baby" or "toddler play ideas," you'll find thousands of complicated suggestions.

Have you ever spent a good part of an hour gathering a bunch of printables, paint, glue, scissors, yarn, colored paper? Then, armed with the step-by-step instructions (#1—Cut along the lines, #2—Punch a hole and thread the yarn . . .), you tried to convince your child to do the "fun toddler activity"? And felt frustrated when your child didn't "get it", so it was really you or your child's nanny who did the activity?

Now, don't get me wrong, these are wonderful activities—for school-age kids and maybe preschoolers. But they're *not* toddler activities.[18]

Many people believe that kids learn only when following an activity guide or lesson plan. But that's not the case. Babies and young kids are constantly learning and making discoveries, whether or not we're aware of it.

This comes as a surprise for many parents. I see moms being made to feel like they're failing if their two-year-olds aren't learning the alphabet, filling out worksheets, attending classes, and making Instagrammable arts and crafts.

Recently, a friend forwarded a post by another mom. The mom shared how her four-year-old is enrolled in reading enrichment classes, math lessons, martial arts, gymnastics, art, and foreign language lessons. SIX different classes, all in addition to the child's schoolwork!

My friend said, "And my kids just play! I'm so ashamed of myself." I told her there's nothing to be ashamed of. Kids need the free play more than they need these "enrichment" activities.

It's sad that we now live in a world where moms feel like bad parents if their kids are "just playing." No wonder there are kids as young as six who are tired and burned out because of this immense pressure.

When I was a child growing up in the 80s, most kids spent plenty of time playing outside. Chinese garter, *patintero* (a game where

---

[18] Discover more in this short video on the stages of developmental play by Caroline Essame, occupational therapist and founder of Developmental Play. When most people think of play, they usually think only of the third and fourth stages (meaning making play and higher play). But before kids can go to this stage, they need to start with the first and second stages (sensory body play and attachment safety play in stage 1, and creative explorative play in stage 2). https://youtu.be/aJoS_zphyXU.

you try to run past other kids who block your way), and *tumbalata* (trying to make a can fall by throwing a slipper or another object at it) are all wonderful games for kids' development. Unlike the organized sports that most people think of today when we say "outdoor play," these games are quite flexible and can be easily adapted to younger kids.

Back in those days, we couldn't watch cartoons for more than an hour a day even if we wanted to, because there simply weren't any more cartoons to watch. Watching videos meant renting a VCR tape and the whole family watching it together. Instead of direct messaging or email, we got nice stationery, handwrote a letter, put it in an envelope, bought a stamp, and dropped it in an actual, physical mailbox. Then we had to wait at least two weeks to get a reply.

I know—sounds primitive, right? Reading this, you probably feel the same way I did when my parents told me they used to ride a *kalesa* (horse-drawn cart) when they were kids. But the wonderful thing is that kids actually *played*.

Today, the American Academy of Pediatrics notes, "Parental guilt has led to competition over who can schedule more 'enrichment opportunities' for their children. As a result, there is little time left in the day for children's free play, for parental reading to children, or for family mealtimes."[19] That's why as pediatricians, we're told to *prescribe* play to our patients.

Isn't it ironic that in our mad dash to give our kids the "best of everything," we end up losing what's most important, and what research consistently shows our kids need? Don't fall into this trap. Even if all you take away from this book is the importance of

---

[19] Yogman et al. 2018. "The Power of Play: A Pediatric Role in Enhancing Development in Young Children." *Pediatrics.*

unstructured play, it will be worth it. You'll save yourself and your child from unnecessary stress.

Part III of this book has many ideas for easy play activities. Don't let the simplicity fool you. They will be much more effective than any worksheet or prepared activity in helping babies and young kids grow up to be smart and successful. And that's good news for busy parents.

Benefits of Free Play

Free play supports learning and inspires creativity

Imaginative play is a very important milestone in early childhood. We may take this skill for granted, but kids need it to help them solve problems, learn to be independent, and build social and emotional skills. When your child describes what he does during imaginative play, you'll also see his language blossom.

If we schedule every moment of our kids' lives and direct all of their play and activities, we may think we're helping them, but we're actually impeding their creativity and imaginative play.

Your toddler is very creative. I'm sure you've seen your child invent an activity many times. That's why no matter how many "toddler activities" you search for on the internet, none of them will top your toddler's own creativity.

Free play builds executive function skills

To be successful in life, kids need to learn "executive function" skills.[20] These include planning, decision making, flexible think-

---

[20] "Executive Function: Skills for Life and Learning" (2012) by the Center on the Developing Child, Harvard University. https://developingchild.harvard.edu/resources/inbrief-executive-function-skills-for-life-and-learning/.

ing, and self-control. The foundation for this starts at a young age, when we allow them to make age-appropriate decisions.

During play, your child can tackle manageable challenges and overcome obstacles on his own. With each new accomplishment, no matter how small it may seem today, he practices the same skills he'll need in the future. He'll also build confidence and see himself as a capable person.

You'll reduce stress for both you and your child

Many kids today live over-scheduled lives. Moms tire of shuttling them from one activity to the other. Remember this: kids need downtime too! It will relieve our pressure from feeling like we always need to keep our kids entertained.

"But my toddler will destroy the house if I allow free play!" This is where we break down one of the myths surrounding independent play. Especially for young kids, free play does not mean allowing them to do anything they want. Rather, it means giving them age-appropriate ways to direct their own play.

Six Ways to Encourage Free Play

Let your child play in a safe space

Create a childproof play area for your kids. The only requirement for a child's play area is that it's safe. There's no need to go overboard designing the "perfect" Pinterest-worthy playroom for your child, or to buy the most intricate and expensive dollhouse or kitchen set you can find. In fact, an empty cardboard box may do even more to stimulate your child's creativity than many of the "must-have" toys that are being marketed to parents today.

Avoid choking hazards for babies and young toddlers. Search the internet for "baby activities" and "toddler activities," and you'll find hundreds of activities with many tiny objects. Colored beads. Pasta shells. Water beads (often called "magic beads") that can be especially dangerous if your child swallows them, since they can inflate and block your child's intestines.

I'm not saying this to scare you or to take your child's fun away. These things are so hyped up on the internet that you may get FOMO (fear of missing out) if your child doesn't play with them. But you don't need them to have fun.

Contrary to what some may think, being conscious about safety will foster a child's independence and help make play more fun. Take care of safety basics so you can worry less and focus on the enjoyable part.

Certain toys are NOT safe and shouldn't be given to babies and young kids. You should avoid:

- Walkers.[21] Many babies and young toddlers have died in walker injuries. They also do nothing to help your baby learn to walk, and may even delay walking. A better way to help a child who's just learning to walk is to allow her to hold on to sturdy pieces of furniture such as a sofa or a bed.

- Trampolines should be used only with kids who are at least six years of age, and only in supervised settings with trained

---

[21] "Baby Walkers: A Dangerous Choice" by the American Academy of Pediatrics. https://www.healthy-children.org/English/safety-prevention/at-home/Pages/Baby-Walkers-A-Dangerous-Choice.aspx.

personnel. This means you shouldn't have a trampoline at home or in your child's playroom.[22]

- Anything that has parts that are small enough to fit in your child's mouth. You can use the cardboard tube in the middle of a toilet paper roll as a rough guide. If the toy or any of its parts will fit in the tube, it is a potential choking hazard.[23]

- Here are examples of potential choking hazards: small balls and marbles, balloons, small hair bows and barrettes, pen or marker caps, button type batteries, refrigerator magnets, and beads.[24]

Encourage different ways of playing, including play with open-ended toys and play without toys

Open-ended toys are those that your child can play with in many ways. Examples of open-ended toys are blocks, rainbow arcs, connecting blocks, stuffed animals, magnetiles, musical instruments, common objects such as spoons or bowls, or items from nature, such as leaves.

Have you ever spent good money on what you thought was a great toy, only to find that your toddler is more interested in the box or the wrapper? That's because cardboard boxes and wrappers are open-ended toys too.

---

[22] "Trampolines: What You Need to Know" by the American Academy of Pediatrics. https://www.healthychildren.org/English/safety-prevention/at-play/Pages/Trampolines-What-You-Need-to-Know.aspx.

[23] "How to Buy Safe Toys" by the American Academy of Pediatrics. https://www.healthychildren.org/English/safety-prevention/at-home/Pages/How-to-Buy-Safe-Toys.aspx.

To learn more, go to toddlertalkingbook.com and access the online resources that come with this book. I've included a guide on babyproofing and childproofing.

[24] "Choking Prevention" by the American Academy of Pediatrics. https://www.healthychildren.org/English/health-issues/injuries-emergencies/Pages/Choking-Prevention.aspx.

Compared to close-ended toys (such as shape sorters, stacking rings or push-button toys), your child is less likely to outgrow open-ended toys because he can play with them in different ways as he grows older.

Let's take wooden blocks, for example. A baby who's four to five months old may start by grasping and exploring them. A toddler may try stacking them, stamping them on Play Doh, or tossing them in the air. A child who's nearing the age of three may pretend that a block is anything from a car to a castle to food for his toy giraffe.

There are three things I want to emphasize. First, it's not about the toy, but how it's used. For example, there's nothing to stop your child from doing pretend play with the shapes in the shape sorter or singing along with the music from a push-button toy. You'll see how your child can take any ordinary object—a box, a blanket, your hair tie—and turn it into a toy.

Second, there's no such thing as a "must have" toy. The internet is full of lists of "10 toys your one-year-old must have," or "20 toys your two year old needs right now." These are marketing hype. There's nothing magical about these toys. There should be absolutely no guilt on your part if your child doesn't have everything that people say he should.

Third, play without toys is just as important! This allows your child to practice pretend play and stimulates creativity.

> It's not about the toy, but how it's used.

Minimize directions

Instead of telling your child how to play, let your child take the lead. Maybe you're trying to follow an activity guide about making a clay representation of an animal farm. But your child is just making blobs of clay that he says are animals and wants to pretend they're talking with each other.

That's okay! That's what play is supposed to be. Resist the urge to correct him and say, "No, that's not how to do it," then reshape the animals and arrange them so they look exactly like the photo in the activity guide.

Instead of directions, you can help spark creativity by demonstrating some fun ideas. For example, you can have some of her stuffed animals talk with each other, or you can demonstrate building different structures with your child's Lego Duplo.

And when your child makes a mess or breaks something, that's okay too. Toddlers who make a mess or break a toy are not being naughty. They *need* to pass through the stage where they can simply explore and make a mess. [17]

Avoid overstimulation

Children can feel overwhelmed if they have too many toys to choose from. Set up a toy rotation so that not all of your child's toys are out at the same time. This also keeps things interesting. When you bring a toy out of rotation, it's as if your child has a new toy. (The time will come when your child realizes where you keep the toys that are "out of rotation" and remember them even if he hasn't seen them in weeks. This will lead to some interesting conversations!)

Also, don't stress about decorating your child's play area with "educational" posters. Many parents feel the need to cover the walls with numbers, the alphabet, or the life cycles of insects.

However, an environment like this may actually disrupt attention and interfere with learning.[25] So save your time and effort. Just keep the walls plain, or add family photos if you wish.

Go outdoors

Nature stimulates your child's development in a way that not even the best indoor play area can replicate. When kids play outside, they learn more, behave better, and are mentally and physically healthier.[26]

Tragically, many kids today don't get enough time outdoors. If many cities, it's tough to find open spaces where kids can run freely, safely, and without breathing in polluted air. That's why we need to advocate for more outdoor play areas. If have a choice on where to live, consider this strongly when making your decision.

Allow down time

The internet is full of ideas on how parents can "keep kids occupied" all throughout their waking hours. Our society today is so allergic to boredom. Heaven forbid our kids become unoccupied for any chunk of time! Because of this, parents feel immense pressure to constantly "provide play activities" for their kids, or to hand over a gadget the moment a child seems bored.

Of course, as I mentioned earlier, we don't advocate leaving babies alone in their cribs all day or strapped into strollers staring into space. But neither should we micro-schedule every minute of a

[25] Fisher, et al. 2014. "Visual Environment, Attention Allocation, and Learning in Young Children: When Too Much of a Good Thing May Be Bad." *Psychological Science.*
[26] "Playing Outside: Why It's Important for Kids." American Academy of Pediatrics. https://www.healthychildren.org/English/family-life/power-of-play/Pages/playing-outside-why-its-important-for-kids.aspx.

child's waking hours. So don't worry if there are times your child seems to be "doing nothing."

At first, it may feel impossible to just have down time. It may seem like the moment you don't provide a toy or activity, she'll do something she's not supposed to—like strip off your wallpaper or eat the dust balls under your bed.

If that happens, go to the ideas in part III of this book. Redirect your child to what's okay for her to do. With practice, your child will gradually learn to appreciate down time and be less dependent on you for constant entertainment. Life will be less stressful for you, your child, and your family.

Take Action Today

> Take ten minutes to just sit and watch your child play. Don't worry about what he should be learning. Just let him play. If you do this every day, you'll be amazed at how your child comes up with hundreds of play ideas!

CHAPTER 5

READ TO YOUR CHILD

> *"Even the youngest babies love to be held close and hear the voice of a loved one as they read a book aloud. These experiences create strong parent-child bonds and impart a sense of well-being and safety. They also promote healthy brain growth, including positive emotional and social development."*
>
> **—Reach Out and Read**

READING WITH YOUR child is one of the best ways to introduce her to the beauty and complexity of language. Your child learns new words and discovers how they're used in context. She builds her listening comprehension skills.

Books also pave the way for other language-boosting activities. Pretending to be the characters. Talking about the stories.

Reading to your child helps them build more than just language skills. By focusing on you and the book, he starts learning how to pay attention. Books can help him talk about and understand emotions. You can also read books to make parts of your routine easier, such as taking a bath, brushing teeth, or pottying.

The most important benefit is the connection with you. Seeing your face as you read the story. Hearing your voice, along with the intonation and emotions behind it. Getting a hug when the story is over. It's a special bonding time.

Reading with your child is not the same as teaching your child how to read. As we emphasize throughout this book, the baby and toddler years are not the time to teach your child to read.

However, it's never too early to read to your baby. A lot of the research on reading to babies and young kids was conducted under the Reach Out and Read Program.[27] In this program, doctors encourage parents to read to their kids and provide age-appropriate books as early as when babies are two months old. Kids who took part in the program did better in tests of language development and also had improved school readiness.

I often work with parents for whom English is not their first language, and they often worry that they're not good enough readers or English speakers. They think it's better to let their kids watch YouTube videos instead. But this isn't true. In these research studies, even if a parent didn't speak English well or isn't a native English speaker, kids still got the same benefits.[28]

When it comes to reading to your child, not even the most famous audiobook narrator can be better than you.

---

[27] When parents are encouraged to read to their babies and toddlers, children's language development improves by 3-6 months. This page summarizes the evidence on the Reach out and Read program. https://reachoutandread.org/why-we-matter/the-evidence/.

[28] Klass, et al. 2009. "Reach Out and Read: Literacy Promotion in Primary Care." *Advances in Pediatrics.*

Tips for Reading To Your Child

Choose a variety of books

Many books marketed for babies and young kids just show a picture and a word, and don't have a narrative. I feel these books are actually just flash cards bound together. Because of this, many parents think that "reading to your baby" actually means drilling baby on these words.

Don't limit yourself to these "flashcard books"! There are so many other books that can make your reading time richer and more enjoyable. There are books with stories, books with facts, books that teach lessons outright and books that seem to be just for fun but really do have lessons. Books with poems and rhymes, and books that are just pictures.

If your family uses more than one language at home, it's also great to have books in each of these languages. I've included a list of my favorite books in the online resources that come with this book.

Choose print books over e-books

For babies and young kids, there's no substitute for holding a book in their hands. This means a book they can actually feel, turn the pages of—and even bite!

Cloth and board books are great for babies. Plastic books also make a great bath time toy. Your baby doesn't really put "books" and "toys" in different categories. For your baby, they're all things she can have fun with. That's why, whether you introduce a book or a toy, your baby will explore it in different ways, like shaking, turning it around, and even dropping it to the floor.

Board books are great for toddlers too. Pages of board books are easier for little hands to turn, and you won't need to worry about them tearing the pages. As your child nears the age of three and develops more finger dexterity, you may try introducing picture books with paper pages.

We have so many choices for baby and toddler books. Lift the flap books. Pop up books. Books with different textures. Books that make sounds or have plastic buttons your child can push. Books with toys or musical instruments attached. Busy books with lots of activities. And many others.

You don't need to go overboard and buy every kind of book there is. A few well-chosen books are all you need. You can even get them at reduced prices in book sales, or secondhand from other parents.

Focus on the interaction

More than the actual content of the book, it's the connection and interaction that count. That's why watching a video of a book will never replace us actually reading with our kids.

When reading to your child, sit so that you and your child can see each other, and both of you can see the book. You can do this by cuddling the baby in your lap. Babies love being held and cuddled while being read to.

> More than the actual content of the book, it's the connection and interaction that count.

Once your child can sit independently, try sitting in a "triangle" position. You, your child, and the book will be the "points" of the triangle. Of course, if your child still prefers your lap, that's okay too!

Reading to your child while cuddling him in your lap does wonders for his brain development. (Illustration by Debbie Qua-Aguiling, MD)

Include it in your routine

Try to have a few minutes of reading time most days of the week. Depending on your routine as a family, choose when it would be best to do this.

Leave books in different parts of your house, in places where your child can reach them easily. In this way, books will become part of your child's day without a lot of effort on your part.

Many parents like to read to their kids at bedtime. This is a great way to calm down, and your child can look forward to this before bed every night. If you have a specific set of books you read at bedtime, it can help signal to your baby or toddler that it's time for bed.

Make it fun!

Let the experience be fun and relaxing for you and your child. If you notice that you or your child are no longer enjoying the reading session, stop. Don't worry that you're "breeding bad habits." It's much better to respond to your child's cues.

Don't stress over whether your child is learning or not, whether they're learning the letters of the alphabet as you read, or whether they know all the words in the book. If you start feeling stressed, relax and take a step back. Remind yourself of why you're doing this. Focus on the connection.

Take Action Today

> Cuddle your child on your lap and read a book to her. Try this before bedtime. I find this to be a great calming activity to wind down just before sleep. Even just five minutes doing this will work wonders!

THE "PARENTING MAGIC WAND"

Anna is the busy mom of one-year-old Amanda. Because she wants to do to boost Amanda's development, she's been searching Google and Pinterest for learning activities.

She sets up a promising-looking activity with flour, food coloring, pipe cleaners, and paper cutouts. Amanda spends a couple of minutes happily smearing the flour and food coloring all over the paper cutouts, then grabs the pipe cleaners and bites them. After some struggling, Anna finally manages to pry them out of Amanda's grasp.

Later, while Anna cleans up the mess, Amanda keeps shouting, "Mommy! Mommy!" and demanding attention. All this while, Anna feels stressed and thinks about what other activities and printables she should try next time.

She thinks, "Why does parenting have to be so hard? Isn't there any way—any way at all—that this can be easier?"

"WHAT CAN I do to raise a smarter child?" This is one of the most common questions I hear from parents.

Did you know there's a method you can do in less than five minutes—that is free and easy enough that anyone can do—and that research has shown works wonders for your child's development? Imagine there's *one thing* you can do that is proven by science to help your child be smarter, that will boost your child's brain development, help your child's language skills, and help your child be:

- happier
- healthier
- more successful
- more resilient

Wouldn't you want to do this every day?

Think about it. If this method were to cost two thousand dollars—and was proven, with benefits, and you had the money to spend, wouldn't you buy it?

Now what if I told you—not only is it proven, not only does it have powerful benefits—but it's also *free*, what would you say?

"Too good to be true!" You might say. These sound like internet marketing scams and false claims. But it's not. Research proved this method at the Center on the Developing Child at Harvard University.[29]

What is it? It's not what many would want you to think. It has nothing to do with a special technique to introduce academics

---

[29] "Serve and Return," Center on the Developing Child, Harvard University. https://developing-child.harvard.edu/science/key-concepts/serve-and-return/.

early. It's also very simple to do—much simpler than any of the "toddler activities" on the internet.

It's so simple and it benefits every aspect of your child's life and your relationship with her, that I like to call it the *parenting magic wand*. If you make the time to do this every day with your child from a young age, it will help in everything from language development to tantrums to overall behavior.

This powerful magic wand is called *serve and return*.[30]

What are serve and return interactions? Just like a game of tennis where the players hit a ball back and forth, during serve and return, you and your child keep the interaction going back and forth.

Here are the five steps for serve and return:[31]

1. Your child will look or point at something, or say something. This is called the "serve." A "serve" can happen when your child looks or smiles at you, looks at something, points to something, or says something. Notice the serve.

2. "Return" the serve by supporting and encouraging. Look at where your child is pointing. Smile back.

3. Smile and make a comment. You can also repeat what your child says. If what your child says is not that clear, you can repeat it back in a clearer way.

4. Pause and allow your child to respond.

---

[30] This is one of my favorite videos about serve and return. Seven-year-old Molly Wright explains it so well! https://www.youtube.com/watch?v=aISXCw0Pi94.

[31] "How-to: 5 Steps for Brain-Building Serve and Return," Center on the Developing Child, Harvard University https://developingchild.harvard.edu/resources/how-to-5-steps-for-brain-building-serve-and-return/.

5. Practice endings and beginnings. Notice when your child's attention has moved to something else—such as when your child looks away or moves toward something else. This last step is very important! We need to recognize the cues that our kids are ready to end an activity. Too often we get frustrated because we try to push a child to do an activity even if they're giving all the cues that they're ready to end it.

Here's an example:

Your child hears a truck pass by outside. He points to the window. You go with him to the window. You smile at him and look at what he is pointing. He gestures and talks.

He says, "Truck!" (And maybe a lot of other things—only half may be understandable to you.)

You say, "Yes, that's a big truck! That's the garbage truck that picks up the garbage from our neighborhood."

> With serve and return interactions, you'll supercharge your child's brain development while enjoying the experience.

You pause and let your child respond. After a few minutes, the truck moves away and your child shifts attention to something else. You respond to your child's shift in attention by going with him too.

Practice serve and return when you talk, play, or read with your child. You'll supercharge your child's brain development while enjoying the experience even more.

By taking small moments during the day to practice serve and return, you build the foundation for your child's lifelong learning, behavior, and health.

I'd like to share my personal experience with this. Earlier, I mentioned how I second-guessed myself as a mom. When I talk about that mom who spends hours searching for activities, downloading and preparing them—I know, because that used to be me!

I personally experienced gathering ten different materials (glue, glitter, flour, three bins, food coloring, and more) while my baby was screaming, "Mommy, mommy," wanting me to play with him.

How ironic is it that I had to ignore my baby to prepare an activity for him? Thankfully, I got a wake-up call from my mentors in developmental and behavioral pediatrics, who reminded me of serve and return interactions.

So, I abandoned the activity guides. I just sat there and looked my baby in the eye. He responded by trying to talk. I repeated some of what he said back to him. Within seconds, he was laughing and squealing in delight! I saw the pure happiness in his eyes.

That's the joy I want you to experience in your parenting.

Anna attended a webinar by a pediatrician that talked about serve and return interactions. She decided to try it.

After the webinar, she stopped searching for activities and put aside the Google drive full of worksheets she'd downloaded. She followed the exact steps to doing serve and return interactions.

She couldn't believe the results. Within the first minute of doing serve and return interactions, Amanda was squealing in delight! Anna is now much happier and less stressed. She finally gets to have the "me time" she badly needs.

Think of all the time saved:

- searching the internet for activities—from 20 minutes to zero
- shopping online for activity supplies—from 30 minutes to 10 minutes (because she now needs fewer things)
- downloading guides, printing worksheets and other printables—from 30 minutes to zero
- preparing for activities—from 30 minutes to zero

That's almost two hours freed up—absolute heaven for a busy parent! Think of what you'd do with all that extra time. Simply enjoy being with your child while doing serve and return. Sleep. Have "me time."

PART III

Your Guide to the First Three Years

CHAPTER 6

YOUR BABY'S FIRST YEAR (0-12 MONTHS)

Mark and Martha are so excited about Matti, their first baby. He's also the first grandchild on both sides of the family. They want to do everything right. They played classical music while Martha was pregnant. They talked to him.

Finally, Matti is here! He's so fragile. He would cry, sleep, poop, and want milk almost constantly. They weren't prepared for the deluge of parenting advice they would get.

"Don't mind him when he cries. You'll spoil him!"

"Let him watch educational videos on YouTube early."

"I saw this video where they're teaching their baby sign language and how to read. You should do that too!"

They're receiving all this advice amid the exhaustion of being new parents. Each time they adjust, it seems like the goalposts change. It feels like they've only just learned to cope with the newborn stage. Then in the blink of an eye, Matti is already rolling over. Before they knew it, he's crawling all over the house.

They wonder what they should do during this time. They feel guilty because they hear some parents are already teaching some lessons during this time, and they're barely keeping up with all they need to do in feeding (then starting solids), dealing with poop and pee, chasing after a crawling baby, and all that goes into new parent territory.

Is there a way to get this parenting thing right, instead of always feeling like I'm failing at something? *Martha wonders.*

THE GOOD NEWS is, yes—there's a way to get this parenting thing right. And it doesn't involve buying expensive programs or getting stressed pushing your baby to do something "advanced."

In this chapter, we'll talk about how to set the stage for your baby's language development. Then we'll go on to simple activities you can do with your baby.

What should your baby be able to do from birth to one year?

Hearing and Understanding	Talking
Birth-3 Months	**Birth-3 Months**
• Startles at loud sounds.	• Makes cooing sounds.
• Quiets or smiles when you talk.	• Cries change for different needs.
• Seems to recognize your voice. Quiets if crying.	• Smiles at people.

4-6 Months

- Moves her eyes in the direction of sounds.
- Responds to changes in your tone of voice.
- Notices toys that make sounds.
- Pays attention to music.

4-6 Months

- Coos and babbles when playing alone or with you.
- Makes speech-like babbling sounds, like pa, ba, and mi.
- Giggles and laughs.
- Makes sounds when happy or upset.

7 Months-1 Year

- Turns and looks in the direction of sounds.
- Looks when you point.
- Turns when you call her name.
- Understands words for common items and people-words like cup, truck, juice, and daddy.
- Starts to respond to simple words and phrases, like, "No", "Come here", and "Want more?"
- Play games with you, like peek-a-boo and pat-a-cake.
- Listens to songs and stories for a short time.

7 Months-1 Year

- Babbles long strings of sounds, like mimi upup babababa.
- Uses sounds and gestures to get and keep attention.
- Points to objects and shows them to others.
- Uses gesture like waving bye, reaching for "up", and shaking his head no.
- Imitates different speech sounds.
- Says 1 or 2 words, like hi, dog, dada, mama, or uh-oh. This will happen around his first birthday, but sounds may not be clear.

Used with permission from the American Speech-Language-Hearing Association.
https://www.asha.org/public/speech/development/01/

Five Ways to Set Up Your Baby for Language Learning Success

Make sure your baby can hear

Every newborn needs a hearing screen. This is already part of standard newborn care in many countries.

If a baby has a hearing problem and we delay in correcting it, the part of the brain responsible for processing sounds won't be able to develop well. So even if we correct the hearing problem later on, if we miss this window of time, the child's language development may be permanently affected.

Appreciate your baby's innate capabilities

In the first chapter I talked about how it's not true that babies "don't know anything," or "don't sense what's going on." Your baby's brain is already actively learning!

During the first year of life, babies are in what psychologist Jean Piaget calls the Sensorimotor Stage, the first of Piaget's four stages of cognitive development. During this stage, babies learn about the world through their senses. They learn how to interact with the world through exploration and experimentation.

An important milestone at nine months is what we call object permanence. This means she understands that things still exist, even if she doesn't see them. She enjoys watching you appear and disappear when you play. That's why she absolutely loves playing peek-a-boo. She also cries when she can't see you, unlike before when she sort of "forgets" you exist when you're out of sight.

So whether your baby is sucking his thumb, playing with his toes, shaking a rattle, or enjoying a game of peek-a-boo—appreciate it! These are all part of cognitive development. To learn more, access the resource library at toddlertalkingbook.com.

Respond to your baby when she cries

Crying is the only way that babies know how to communicate. We want to show them that when they communicate, someone will respond. This communication is the basic foundation for language development.

Soon enough, babies will make sounds other than crying. At around two months old, they'll smile and coo. But even when they're able to make sounds other than crying, or even if they already have their first words, babies and young kids still default to crying when they're upset.

When your baby cries, don't take it personally. It doesn't mean you're a bad parent or you're doing something wrong. While it's not a good idea to consistently ignore baby's crying, you also don't need to panic and rush to fix things each time baby cries.

Breastfeed

Breastfeeding is one of the best things you can do to help your baby's brain and language development. A large and well-conducted study showed that promoting breastfeeding resulted in a 7.5-point advantage in verbal IQ.[32]

I will never shame or judge a mom for not breastfeeding, or for stopping breastfeeding early. Moms need support, not judgment and criticism. If you, in consultation with your pediatrician, decide to introduce milk formula, please don't feel that you've failed.

So why do I include breastfeeding here? Because I often hear parents ask, "What milk will help my child be smarter?" Milk formula is marketed so well that many people feel it's superior and helps babies grow up to be smarter.

If you decide to introduce formula, it should be a decision *you* make in collaboration with your trusted medical team, and not because you felt pressured by someone who kept giving you disapproving stares while saying that your child is "not getting enough milk."

Have plenty of face-to-face time with your baby

Face-to-face time is important at any age, but it's especially important for babies.[33] When babies see how our lips and tongue

---

[32] Kramer, et al. 2008. "Breastfeeding and Child Cognitive Development: New Evidence From a Large Randomized Trial." *Arch Gen Psychiatry.* This study involved more than 17,000 women from 31 hospitals and clinics in Belarus. What's great about this is they didn't simply measure children's IQs then ask whether or not they were breastfed. Instead, this is a randomized controlled trial, considered the best kind of research. In this research, mothers were randomized to receive breastfeeding support through the Baby Friendly Hospital Initiative (BFHI), or the standard intervention at that time. Other than the intervention, the two groups of moms were similar. The study found that the group randomized to BFHI had a mean verbal IQ that was 7.5 points higher.

Horta, et al. 2015. "Breastfeeding and intelligence: A systematic review and meta analysis." *Acta Pediatrica.* In this study, the researchers combined the results of 17 studies on breastfeeding. This research showed that breastfeeding is associated with a 3.44 point increase in IQ (no distinction between verbal and nonverbal IQ).

We're not here to debate the number of IQ points. The point is this—it's not true that formula milk is superior in boosting baby's brain and language development.

[33] Leong, et al. 2017. "Speaker gaze increases information coupling between infant and adult brains." *Proceedings of the National Academy of Sciences.*

move when we talk, look us in the eyes, and watch our facial expressions, they learn not just language but social skills too.

Unfortunately, if we're often glued to our phones and electronic devices, we miss out on face-to-face time. Just think of how much time we spend looking at our phones compared with the faces of the people around us.

If you have a nanny for your baby, I believe it should be a rule not to watch television or be on their phones or gadgets during the time they're "on duty" taking care of your child.

When I tell this to parents, they cry, "That's unreasonable!" Well, hear me out. At a fast-food store, does the cashier post to Instagram while taking your order? How would you feel if a grocery store clerk answers a few messages on her phone while there are people in line? If you enter a bank and the tellers are watching television, would you trust them with your money? Banks, restaurants, grocery stores, and many other places have strict rules saying you can't have phones or gadgets out while serving customers.

At home, your baby is your caregiver's customer. Yes, she can check her phone while she's on break, such as during baby's naps or when someone else is taking care of baby. (That's why your caregiver should have breaks and time off.) But I've seen many caregivers constantly glued to their phones while babies beside them are strapped into strollers. Without anyone to engage with them, the babies either stare blankly into space, halfheartedly swipe at a mobile hung on the stroller, or watch videos on their own gadget.

If you don't have a caregiver and need to work or check your phone for important messages, at least set a time for when you'll check, and limit it to that. You may want to turn on the feature in your phone that allows notifications only from certain people (such as your spouse) and screens out all others. The important thing is during your baby's waking hours, more time should be spent engaging with your baby than using a gadget.

If you feel you haven't been engaging with your baby a lot, take heart. Find the help you need, so you have the time and energy to interact with your baby during her waking hours. I say this with love and without judgment. I know it's difficult and there are a million demands pulling at you a million places at once. But there's a quote that sums this up perfectly:

"Either we spend time with our babies today while they are young, or we spend time later on correcting problems in their development and behavior. Either way, we spend time."

If we'd give anything for our kids – including our lives – can we give up some of our screen time for them?

Language Learning Activities for Your Baby

You don't need complicated activities or expensive toys to help your baby learn language skills. Here are fun things you can do with your baby. If you're already doing these, that's great! You're on the right track.

Talk

1. Sit baby on your lap so she's facing you. Tell her about your day. Sing a soothing song or nursery rhyme.

2. Bring baby around the house and talk to him. Show him what's in the different rooms.

3. Make bath time a fun learning activity. Talk with your baby about what's happening. "I'm getting the shampoo. I'll shampoo your hair now. Aren't these bubbles wonderful? Close your eyes."

4. While feeding your child—whether it's breastfeeding, bottle feeding, or feeding your baby her first solids—look at your baby. Tell her what's happening. Let her respond. Avoid just pushing the milk or the food in her mouth, or just leaving your baby in the crib with a bottle.

5. Observe and respond to your baby's gestures. Unless your doctor or therapist recommends it specifically for your child, there's no need to teach "baby sign language." Your baby will naturally use gestures and imitate yours. This is easier and more powerful than any "baby sign" program out there.

6. Imitate your baby's gestures too. This is sure to get a laugh.

7. Show your baby photos of family members and tell her about them. (Be careful though, especially if they are heirloom photos. If your baby is in the stage where he's grabbing everything, they might get torn.)

8. Spend some time every day doing serve and return interactions. When your baby points at something, look at what he's pointing to. Say something about it. Pause, and wait for him to respond.

9. When she babbles, respond by smiling and talking with her.

10. Talk about the objects in your home as you put them away or get them ready for use. You could say something like, "I'm getting our plates and spoons since it's time to eat."

11. Take your baby to the grocery store and point out objects you need, such as milk, bread, fruit, vegetables, etc.

12. While going for a walk outside together, note the things in your neighborhood. Point them out. Name and describe them.

Play

1. Tummy time is baby's first exercise.[34] During tummy time, go in front of your baby and talk with her too. Give a big smile and show her your facial expression. Holding baby belly-down on your chest is a great way to do tummy time too.

2. Do safe and easy sensory play. The internet makes sensory play seem so complicated. However, many of the things you do every day, like carrying and rocking baby, giving her a bath, and breastfeeding or feeding her a meal are all sensory activities.

3. Show your baby a mirror. Let your baby pat his reflection and observe his own facial expressions. Talk with him as you do this. Make funny faces while looking at your reflections side by side.

4. Play peek-a-boo. If wearing a mask is common where you live, in addition to "regular" peek-a-boo, you can add a variation that includes a mask. Put a mask on, then remove it.[35] This shows your baby that when he sees a person wearing a mask, there's something behind it.

[34] "Back to Sleep, Tummy to Play." American Academy of Pediatrics. https://www.healthychildren.org/English/ages-stages/baby/sleep/Pages/Back-to-Sleep-Tummy-to-Play.aspx.
[35] Green, et al. 2021. "The implications of face masks for babies and families during the COVID 19 pandemic: A discussion paper." *Journal of Neonatal Nursing.*

5. Hide a toy under a cloth and encourage your baby to look for it. Ask, "Where's the toy?" Then when baby finds it, say with a flourish, "There it is!"

When it comes to play, one of the questions I hear most often is, "What toys do I need to buy for baby?"

The best answer to this question really is—NONE. Yes, your baby will be fine even if you don't buy him a single toy! As we often say, YOU are your baby's best "toy" and the only "toy" he really needs.

But if you're looking for toys, here's what I'd recommend:

- Rattle, or something that your or baby can shake to make sounds.

- Toy animals or stuffed animals.

- Open-ended toys such as balls, blocks or rainbow arc toys.

- Books. For babies, books are toys too. They don't yet distinguish between books and toys. Whether it's a book or a toy, it will get grabbed, chewed, thrown to the ground—and all sorts of things.

- Household items—you can use safe household objects as toys. Examples are bowls (the unbreakable kind) and spoons.

- Magazines, scrap paper, and cardboard boxes (check these for dangers such as staple wire or choking hazards).

Read

1. Read to your baby. Use cloth books that you can put in the laundry when they get dirty, or board books you can wipe. Make sure they're clean, since your baby will definitely want to chew on them.

2. Put a few favorite books in a basket and let your baby explore them.

3. Read to your baby in different voices. Exaggerate your gestures. Don't be afraid to act silly. Watch her facial expression and how she responds. When you see her particularly enjoying something, repeat it. When you tailor what you do to how she reacts, you encourage her communication skills.

CHAPTER 7

YOUR ONE-YEAR-OLD (12-23 MONTHS)

Matti just had his first birthday! Mark and Martha are so excited to celebrate this milestone with family and friends. But they weren't prepared for all the questions they heard:

- *"So, will you enroll him in a toddler class?"*
- *"No YouTube? How will he learn?!!"*
- *"Why isn't Matti approaching me?"*

Not to mention all the toddler parenting advice they see on the internet! They're now questioning themselves, Are we doing something wrong? Does Matti really need to approach everyone easily? Do we need to worry about enrolling in classes or letting him watch educational videos?

I T'S YOUR CHILD's first birthday! This is such an exciting time. Your child may have just started taking her first steps. When you give her a set of blocks, she can place one block on top of another.

Your one-year-old can follow one-step commands with gestures. You have so much fun doing this! She can do "beautiful eyes" and "flying kiss." When you say words such as "ball" or "spoon," you'll notice that she looks towards those objects.

Your toddler explores everything about their environment. And I do mean *everything*—even things you don't want them exploring. Everything they see around them, they try to fit into this schema of the world that they're forming in their minds. This develops their vocabulary and language skills.

What should your toddler be able to do at 1-2 years?

Hearing and Understanding	Talking
• Points to a few body parts when you ask. • Follows 1-part directions, like "Roll the ball" or "Kiss the baby." • Responds to simple questions, like "Who's that?" or "Where's your shoe?" • Listens to simple stories, songs, and rhymes. • Points to pictures in a book when you name them.	• Uses a lot of new words. • Uses p, b, m, h, and w in words. • Starts to name pictures in books. • Asks questions, like "What's that?", "Who's that?" and "Where's kitty?" • Puts 2 words together, like "more apple," "no bed," and "mommy book."

Used with permission from the American Speech-Language-Hearing Association. https://www.asha.org/public/speech/development/12/ .

Language Learning Activities for Your One-Year-Old

Talk

1. At this age, your child is starting to follow commands. Make use of this! Give simple commands that she can follow. For example, hold out your arms and say, "Give mommy a hug!"

2. Before you do something, describe what you will do. For example, if you will give your child a drink, don't just place the cup in his mouth. Look at your child and say, "Mommy will give you a drink." Or ask, "Do you want a drink?" Then you can allow him to get the cup and drink, or you can give him a drink. This improves behavior too, because it teaches your child what to expect.

3. When your child is about to explore somewhere off limits, say, "No" and shake your head too. If he doesn't follow, you may need to give a physical prompt by leading him away. Follow up by showing your child where it's okay to explore.

4. Take a walk outside the house and point out trees, birds, leaves, cars—everything is new and interesting to your child. Soon, your child will point too.

5. Your child will naturally point to many things that interest him. When he does, look at the object, then at him. Comment on it and let your child respond. For example, if he looks at your neighbor's dog passing by, you can say, "Yes, that's a big brown dog! Our neighbor is walking her dog."

6. During mealtimes, give your child two or three food choices. Then ask, "Which one do you like? Chicken or broccoli?"

Let him point or get the one that he prefers. Of course, he may want both or neither, and that's fine too.

7. If your child seems to be frustrated because she wants something, encourage her to point to it. You can then lead her nearer to where she is pointing.

8. When meeting friends and loved ones or doing video chat, encourage your child to wave or give a "flying kiss."

9. Continue to describe and point things out when running errands, going for walks, or doing chores around the house. When talking with your child, look at her so that she sees your gestures and facial expression.

10. Look through family photos. Describe what's happening. For example, "That's daddy playing with your Uncle Ed when both of them were kids. Don't they look like they're having such fun?" Pause and give your child time to respond, even if the words aren't clear yet.

11. When going out, particularly if you're going to a new place, describe where you are going, as well as what you will do when you get there. For example, if you will visit an aunt, say something like this: "We're going to your Aunt Betty's house. When we get there, we'll all say hi to her." Demonstrate saying hi, and he may imitate you too.

12. Sing nursery rhymes that involve actions such as, "Hokey Pokey," "Open Shut Them," "I'm a Little Teapot," or "Incy Wincy Spider."

Play

1. When your child is following commands and walking independently, it's a great time to try playing "Bring Me." Start

with common objects such as a ball, spoon, cup, or book. Later on, your child will bring things to you on her own. If she does, comment on them. Or your child may name them herself.

2. Play movement games, and talk while you're playing. For example, lift your child and say "up." Put him down and say "down." Jog a few steps (carefully, of course) while carrying your child or while pushing his stroller and say "fast." Then walk slowly and say "slow." Toddlers love games like these. I know mine does. He'd give a big laugh and say, "Again! Again!"

3. Do finger play with songs such as "Where is Thumbkin", "Finger Family", or "Open Shut Them."

4. Demonstrate simple ways of doing pretend play. Try making your child's stuffed animals talk with each other, or pretend to feed them.

5. At this age, your child enjoys deliberately dropping or throwing toys and other objects. When you pick them up and hand them to her, she'll do it over and over again. She's not being naughty, but this is part of her development. Instead of scolding, direct your child to *what* and *where* they can throw. Describe what you're both doing, so it becomes an opportunity for language learning.[36]

Great toys for this age

- Nesting toys and shape sorters
- Large crayons and paper
- Connecting toys

---

[36] Want to read more about why toddlers throw toys, and what to do about it? Check out this article. https://discerningparenting.com/toddler-throw-toys/.

- Simple child-size musical instruments such as a drum or maracas
- Bath toys (boats, containers)
- Boxes and paper tubes
- Dolls, trucks, trains, stuffed animals, pretend tools or kitchen utensils and other items for pretend play. These don't have to be elaborate. You don't need that exquisite doll house with collector items, which will leave you frustrated when your toddler breaks something.
- Ball pit
- Outdoor toys such as slides, swings, and sandboxes

Read

Read a picture book together with your child. Point to the pictures. Encourage your child to point to the pictures too. This is a great age for pointing out characters and objects in books.

Mark and Martha did exactly these things mentioned above throughout Matti's second year. They felt more relaxed and confident. They didn't need to worry about classes or reading lessons, or rush to entertain him all the time. They found Matti slowly becoming more independent and able to play creatively with his toys. Of course, now that they're entering the second year, it's a whole new game as Matti is running faster and they're seeing those toddler tantrums. But they're confident that with the relationship they've built, as well as Matti's budding language skills, they can joyfully handle the next stage.

CHAPTER 8

YOUR TWO-YEAR-OLD (24-36 MONTHS)

Mark and Martha's neighbors, Ted and Teresa, have a two-year-old daughter, Tammy. Teresa has read many parenting books and she follows all the parenting bloggers she can find on Instagram. She is feeling confused, and she thinks to herself, Should I enroll Tammy in online classes? I saw that mom in the parenting group. She posted a video that her 18-month-old can already read. But I haven't even started teaching Tammy the alphabet! I'm such a bad mom. Also, Tammy is having tantrums! But she can already talk. Why can't she just tell me what she wants instead of screaming?

The Preoperational Stage: Why You Can't Reason with Your Two-Year-Old

"IF YOU'D JUST done what I told you to do thirty minutes ago, we'd be done by now and you'd be playing!" You explain this several times, but all your toddler does is give a cheeky grin. Is she being naughty and hardheaded?

No, she's simply in what Piaget calls the "preoperational stage" of development. There are three key characteristics of this stage.

First, kids this age have difficulty with logical thinking. If you've tried to reason with a toddler, you know what I mean! Logical thinking starts during the concrete operational stage, which is usually around seven years of age. Even further away is the formal operational stage, where they learn abstract concepts. This doesn't come until they become teenagers.

That's why, when telling your child what to do, be concrete and specific. Often, we love telling young kids, "Behave!" But what does "behave" mean? This is an abstract concept that toddlers have difficulty understanding.

So, for example, if you want your child to "behave" instead of hitting a table with his toy dinosaur, say, "Toys are not for hitting. It's more fun to make your dino jump or do a dino dance!" Or better yet, model it.

Another important characteristic of the preoperational stage is pretend play. Your child is learning to use symbols. For example, he may pretend that a block can be anything from a phone to a truck or even food for a stuffed animal. Pretend play is a very important milestone, and is important too in building language skills.

The third characteristic is called egocentrism, which means that your toddler has a difficult time taking on someone else's perspective. Help your toddler with this by talking about how other people are thinking and feeling.

What should your toddler be able to do at 2-3 years?

Hearing and understanding	Talking
• Understands opposites, like go-stop, big-little, and up-down. • Follows 2-part directions, like "Get the spoon and put it on the table." • Understands new words quickly.	• Has a word for almost everything. • Talks about things that are not in the room. • Uses k, g, f, t, d, and n in words. • Uses words like in, on, and under. • Uses two- or three-words to talk about and ask for things. • People who know your child can understand him. • Asks, "Why?" • Puts 3 words together to talk about things. May repeat some words and sounds.

Used with permission from the American Speech-Language-Hearing Association.
https://www.asha.org/public/speech/development/23/.

Language Learning Activities for Your Two-Year-Old

Talk

1. Take a walk around. Point to objects and ask, "What's this?" Or ask him to describe what he sees. Do this in a fun and conversational way, and not like you're giving your child a quiz. Before long, your child will also keep asking, "What's this?" Constantly! :)

2. Continue having conversations with your child. During play, give a big smile and ask your child, "What are you doing?" Let your child respond, then comment on what your child says.

3. Ask your child to complete the lines of poems or stories that your child knows well. Say, "Humpty Dumpty sat on the..." and let your child answer, "wall!" Soon, your child will tell the stories and reciting the rhymes and songs too.

4. Ask silly questions. For example, get your child's shirt and ask, "Is this mommy's shirt?" Then pretend to wear it. Or point to his tummy and ask, "Is this [child's name]'s foot?" This is sure to get many laughs!

5. Look through photos together and take turns describing what is happening. Try asking questions about emotions such as, "How do you think I'm feeling in this picture?"

6. At the end of the day, ask your child questions like, "What did we do today?" You can eventually move on to questions like, "What are you most grateful for today?" At this age, your child may not really talk about what happened today, but will say something that happened yesterday or even last week. That's okay! Respond by saying something like, "Oh yes, we went to the park yesterday. Wasn't that fun!"

7. Talk about your child's feelings. Label feelings when you notice them. Say something like, "You seem upset right now." Simply describe what's happening, instead of denying it with statements like, "There's nothing to be upset about. You should be happy!"

8. If your child does something you don't agree with but isn't harmful, instead of stopping him immediately, try asking

why. You may be surprised that what he has in mind isn't misbehavior at all. This has happened to me several times. One time, I was opening a package, when my son suddenly went to my husband's desk. I thought he was going to mess up dad's things! (Turns out, he wanted to get a pair of scissors to help me).

9. As your child nears age three, she'll start asking lots of questions. And I do mean *a lot of questions*. Constantly. You don't need to answer all of them. For some questions, you can say, "What do you think?" This engages their critical thinking skills, too.

10. Model gratitude, respect, kindness and empathy in how you talk. This goes for any age. Soon, your child will follow your example.

Play

1. Take turns describing what the other will draw. For example, if your child says, "Santa Claus," draw Santa Claus (any blob that sort of looks like Santa will do). When he says, "reindeer" or "sleigh," add them to the drawing. This was one of my child's favorite activities.

2. Play a simple game of "charades." Take turns pretending to do something and guessing what the other is doing. You and your child may not get the answers right, but you'll have lots of fun.

3. Make a game out of creating your own rhymes. Don't worry if they're obviously made up and are nothing like the rhymes we read in books. Personally, I've said things like, "Let's eat our porridge, and later on let's draw a bridge." Or while

picking out clothes, "Let's choose a shirt to wear, one that doesn't have a bear." How ridiculous are these?! But my son loves this game, and it never fails to amuse him.

4. While your child is playing, tell him to describe what he's doing. You'll be surprised what creative ideas he comes up with!

5. Play games that involve imitation such as "Follow the Leader." Your toddler will also enjoy games that involve timing large movements with song lyrics, such as "Ring Around the Rosie."

Great toys for this age

- Wooden blocks and connecting toys are a great staple for any age! You'll notice that your child can do more with them. Try introducing blocks with different shapes and colors, and asking your child to sort them by shape or color.

- Crayons, paint, and sheets of paper. Plain sheets of paper (or even scrap paper and cardboard boxes) are better than worksheets or printables.

- Rainbow arcs

- Play dough

- Simple jigsaw puzzle

- Musical instruments such as a toy keyboard

- Items for pretend play such as dolls and animal figures are great for this age too. You'll see how your child's made-up stories become more complex as she grows.

- Outdoor toys such as slides, swings, and sandboxes

- Child-size tricycle

Read

1. Books with rhymes are great for this age. I love the Dr. Seuss Books for this. They have a great cadence for reading aloud, and are lots of fun too.

2. Try different variations during your reading time. On some days, just read the story as is. Other times, take turns describing the pictures with your toddler. If it's a familiar story, ask your toddler to tell you parts of it. Ask questions like, "So what happened next?"

3. When reading, ask questions that involve understanding emotions and perspective taking. For example, "How do you think Dorothy felt when she realized she's not in Kansas anymore?" Make it fun. There's no pressure on your child to give essay-quality answers.

Building Your Child's Word Bank

As your child goes through what we call the "language explosion," we want to see them use a variety of words too. We also want to see kids combining these words in a variety of ways to communicate with others. Here are activities to help your child develop a vocabulary in each of these categories.

Nouns

These are usually among the first words your child learns, even before age two. Most of your child's vocabulary will be things she encounters every day. If you read with your child regularly, her vocabulary will also include what she reads about. As your child nears age three, she'll be forming mental categories of these, such as classifying them into people, animals, food, toys, or clothes.

Pronouns

At around this age, your child will start using pronouns. Before this age, she'll refer to you as "mommy" and use her name to refer to herself. After your child turns two, she'll gradually use "you" and "I/me."

Ask questions that involve pronouns. For example, at bedtime, ask, "Do you want to turn off the lights, or do you want me to do it?"

Prepositions

Let your child help you with errands. Include commands with prepositions such as, "Put the carton of milk on the table," or "Please put the butter inside the refrigerator."

Get a box and a few toys (such as a truck, stuffed toy, or animal figure). For example, say, "Doggie is inside the box." Then, "Doggie has jumped outside the box!" (while doing the corresponding action).

Pretend play with a large cardboard box. Say, "[Child's name] is inside the box." "Oh, now you're outside the box!" Get a toy, put it under the box and say, "Your truck is under the box."

Verbs

Practice your child's language skills, build self-esteem, and get some help too! Give two-step commands such as, "Wash your hands, then help me put the vegetables on the counter."

Play a simple version of "Simon Says." Use two-step commands like, "Simon says—wave your hands and give a kick." or "Turn in a circle and say hello." (Forget the rule that you shouldn't do it if there's no "Simon Says." That's too complicated for this age.)

Play "Bring Me." Your child will enjoy bringing the things you request, and also things that she wants you to see. It's fun for the whole family.

When reading together, point to a picture and ask your child, "What are they doing?"

Adjectives

These are part of expected developmental milestones at around age three, but go ahead and start using them even early on.

When your child says something, expand on it. For example, if she says, "Ice cream!" Say, later "Yes, ice cream is quite yummy, isn't it?" You can do this at any age, and with any vocabulary level.

Show pictures of faces with different emotions and ask her to name them. If your child had a tantrum, after she calms down, ask, "How did you feel?" Take the time to listen.

Take opportunities throughout the day to use adjectives. For example, when your child tries to carry a heavy object, you can say, "Be careful, that's heavy!"

Numbers—in real life

Don't stress too much about whether or not your toddler can count one to twenty by rote. The expected developmental milestone for counting is "counts to three at thirty months." It's more important that he understands the concepts of numbers, and that he hears numbers being used in conversation and in everyday life.

Take opportunities to use numbers during everyday activities. Let's say you're having cookies. Ask, "Would you like one or two pieces?" When packing away toys or books, count them. You can also count things in the pictures of the books you read.

You don't need to be conscious about the age that you use two-step commands, prepositions, or any of the developmental milestones in the previous section. You can use these words at any age. Just converse with your child.

> *Interactive communication* is the most important language skill to develop at this age; *not* reciting things by rote.

I cannot emphasize this enough. *Interactive communication* is the most important language skill to develop at this age; *not* reciting things by rote.

PART IV

Special Considerations

CHAPTER 9

SCREEN TIME AND LANGUAGE DEVELOPMENT

WHAT'S THE ONE topic that sparks more heated debates and mommy wars than any other? Screen time. Any mention of possible bad effects of screen time is labeled as "parent shaming."

I assure you, this discussion is not about parent shaming. Rather, it's about empowering you and helping you decide what's best.

Let's start by defining the kind of screen time we're talking about. This is time a child spends on any device—whether it's a television, a computer, or a handheld device such as a mobile phone or a tablet. Watching videos, using "learning apps," playing games, or even viewing a PowerPoint presentation of the alphabet are all included in "screen time."

An exception is video chat. Going on Face Time or Zoom and chatting with the grandparents or with other kids is a great way to connect! So when we say, "no screen time for babies below eighteen months," it doesn't mean your baby can't have a video chat with Grandma.

It feels as if we are fighting a losing battle if we try to limit our kids' gadget time. Gadgets are everywhere. A 2021 study conducted by Kaspersky showed that 48 percent of kids spend an average of three to five hours a day on a digital device. Eleven percent of kids already have their own gadget even before the age of five.[37]

It gets worse as the kids grow older. Another study by the Kaiser Family Foundation found that kids age eight to eighteen were spending over seven and a half hours a day on a screen for entertainment.[38] This means that every year, kids spend a full 118 days—practically one third of their life—in front of a screen!

When my child was a baby, I heard comments such as, "You don't allow your baby to watch YouTube? How will he learn? He'll be behind other kids! He'll be left out when he goes to school and he doesn't know what's popular."

I assure you, what's popular when your child is a baby will be old news by the time he goes to school. Missing screen time as a baby won't make your child "left out."

"You can't raise a screen free child now. Your child needs to keep up with technology."

If you're a parent reading this book, I'll bet you were already a teenager when you first used an iPad. I'm also pretty sure you

[37] "Raising the smartphone generation: New research into how parents and children manage their digital habits." https://www.kaspersky.com/blog/digital-habits-report-2021/.
[38] "Daily media use among children and teens up dramatically from five years ago." https://www.kff.org/racial-equity-and-health-policy/press-release/daily-media-use-among-children-and-teens-up-dramatically-from-five-years-ago/.

quickly figured out how to use it. Your child will learn whatever technology comes up when he needs it, even if you didn't give him an iPad when he was a baby.

"There's no point limiting gadgets. You'll end up giving in eventually."

Yes, when the time is right, we can choose to let him have some screen time. But not now. Not when he's a baby.

So why bother limiting screen time?

Here's why we need to make the effort, even if it's a huge challenge. Here's why, if we delay introducing screen time as much as we can, it does make a difference.[42]

MRI studies have shown that too much screen time may actually harm the connections forming in your child's brain.[39] I think that if we all had MRI machines and we could SEE with our own eyes what's happening in our kids' brains—we'd be much more careful about screen time.

Excess screen time also screws up the balance of chemicals in the brain, not unlike the effects of drugs such as cocaine.[40] As an addiction expert says, "Giving your child a smartphone is like giving him a gram of cocaine."[41]

[39] Hutton, et al. 2019. "Associations between screen-based media use and brain white matter integrity in preschool-aged children." *JAMA Pediatrics.*
[40] https://www.mayoclinichealthsystem.org/hometown-health/speaking-of-health/are-video-games-and-screens-another-addiction.
[41] https://www.independent.co.uk/news/education/education-news/child-smart-phones-cocaine-addiction-expert-mandy-saligari-harley-street-charter-clinic-technology-teenagers-a7777941.html.

Research shows kids who spend a lot of time on screens tend to have:

- Less well-developed parts of the brain, including the parts needed for language, literacy and emotional regulation.[39]

- Weaker language skills[42] and lower scores on language processing, vocabulary and literacy tests.[39]

- Greater chances of being diagnosed with language and cognitive delays.[43]

These are on top of other effects such as poorer sleep, increased risk of diseases associated with a sedentary lifestyle, and eye problems.[44] Our pediatric eye doctors tell us they now commonly see in young kids the same diseases that they used to see only in the elderly!

My book, The Discerning Parent's Guide to Toddler Behavior: From Power Struggles to Connection, has more about the effects of screen time on your child's behavior, as well as more tips on what we can do to protect our kids.

---

[42] While many researches show that screen time has a negative effect on language development especially for young kids, some may have conflicting results. That's why it's great to combine the results from multiple studies, such as what was done by Madigan, et al. 2020. "Associations between screen use and child language skills: A systematic review and meta analysis." *JAMA Pediatrics.*

This combined the results of 42 research studies that included a total of 20,000 children. More screen time and having the television on in the background were associated with weaker language skills. Protective factors include a later onset of screen use, selecting better-quality educational programs, and co-viewing with a responsible adult.

[43] Birken, et al. 2017. "Handheld screen time linked with speech delays in young children." *Pediatric Academic Societies Meeting.* In this research that included 894 children from 6 months to 2 years of age, each 30-minute increase in handheld screen time was linked to a 49% increase of expressive speech delay.

[44] Lissak G. 2018. "Adverse physiological and psychological effects of screen time on children and adolescents: Literature review and case study." *Environ Res.*

Screen Time Research

Some experts claim there's "very little evidence" that screen time is harmful for babies and young kids. They say these studies only show *correlation*, but there's no proof that screen time *caused* these effects.

Well, to be able to conclusively *prove* that screen time *caused* these, researchers must conduct an experiment. They need to get two groups of young kids. For the experiment to be accurate, these should be large groups that are as similar as possible at the start of the experiment. Then one group should have more than an hour of screen time a day, while the other group has less.

The researchers must also monitor the kids to be sure that the "less screen time" group doesn't sneak in more screen time on some days. Or that the "more screen time" group doesn't suddenly decide not to have less screen time. This experiment must also go on for some time, possibly years. Can you see why this is practically impossible? Not to mention, with all the screen time research that is already out, it would be cruel and unethical.

I predict that a time will come in the future—maybe decades from now—when the link between the harmful effects of excessive screen time on brain and language development of young kids will be just as strong as the link between smoking and cancer.

More than fifty years ago, people were still debating whether or not smoking really causes cancer. Today, it's accepted that smoking does cause cancer and a host of other diseases. We may see media reports of smokers who live to be a hundred. Or we know people who never smoked but still got cancer. But no one uses these stories as "proof" that smoking doesn't harm your health.

If we wait for "more evidence" before we decide to limit screen time, it will be too late for your child. Just as decades ago it was too late for all those people who got cancer from smoking. Don't let your child be the experiment. Do what you can to follow the guidelines that are based on the current evidence we do have.

Screen Time Recommendations by Age[45]

18 Months and Younger

At this age, we recommend not giving them any screen time at all other than video chat.

Some parents feel they need screen time to pacify a crying baby. However, if you do this, you'll only make it harder for yourself as your baby grows. The screen time will actually hurt your baby more than the crying will.

Screen Time for 18 Months to 2 Years

As much as possible, try to delay introducing screen time. At this age, kids need to move around and interact with the real, physical world.

If your toddler watches any television, choose high quality educational programming and avoid solo use of screen media. Watch with him. Talk with him about what he's watching.

---

[45] World Health Organization (2019). "Guidelines on physical activity, sedentary behavior and sleep for children under 5 years of age."

Screen Time for 2 through 5 Years

From two to five years, screen time can be an occasional treat, but try to limit this to an hour or less per day. As much as possible, continue watching together. Talk with your child about what she sees on the screen and help her apply it to the real world.

Where did the one-hour-a-day recommendation come from? Some people on the internet claim it's just a number that "experts made up out of thin air." But there's actual research evidence behind this recommendation. Young kids who had more than an hour a day of screen time were: [46]

- Less curious and less eager to learn new things.
- Less able to calm down.
- More easily distracted.
- More likely to have tantrums and have more difficulty with self-control.

Since the COVID pandemic, some experts feel it's okay to be a bit loose on the screen time recommendations. So if your child goes a little beyond an hour on some days, don't beat yourself up and feel as if you've "lost the screen time battle."

5 Ways to Use Screen Time Wisely

Choose the right type of screen time

Not all screen time is created equal. Choose videos that are the same pace as real life and have fewer scene changes. In the online

---

[46] Twenge and Campbell. 2018. "Associations between screen time and lower psychological well-being among children and adolescents: Evidence from a population-based study." *Preventive Medicine Reports.*

resources that come with this book, I compare two videos—one that is fast paced with lots of scene changes, and another that is the same pace as real life and has fewer scene changes. You'll be surprised that many of the popular "educational" YouTube channels don't fit the criteria for "high quality" screen time.

A television that you control is better compared with a handheld device like a phone or a tablet. Avoid games, including those marketed as "baby learning apps." Even an app that seems educational—like one that flashes stars when your baby taps the right letter on the screen—can be extremely addictive at this age.

I also prefer videos that have real people in them, rather than animations. Say you want your child to watch a video of *The Very Hungry Caterpillar*. Instead of the animated version, it's better to choose a video of a person actually reading the book, flipping the pages and holding the book up for your child to see. Yes, that means those low-tech videos are actually better!

If your child is already used to animations and fast-paced videos, he may protest at first, but give it some time and he'll adjust to calmer screen time.

If your child will use a phone or tablet, instead of using one of those "baby learning apps," try these:

- Take photos with the camera.
- Look at pictures you've taken. However, avoid photo viewing apps with automatic effects such as lots of animations and flashing lights.
- Listen to a story on audio, or listen to music.

- Follow along with exercise and activity videos, such as videos of other kids dancing or doing arts and crafts (as long as they're not too complicated).

Watch with your kids

Research shows that kids who have more unsupervised screen time are "more likely to have suspected deficits in attention, intelligence, and social skills" compared to those whose screen time is supervised.[47]

That's why we recommend you watch with your kids. Try the same triangle position that you use for reading. Sit beside your child with the screen in front of you, and turn to face her a little so she can see your face. Talk with your child about what you're watching.

Turn off when not in use

Keep the TV off when you're at home and no one is watching. In a very interesting study, for EACH HOUR that a television is on in the background, babies and toddlers heard 770 fewer words from the adults around them.[48]

This can hinder their language development. Remember the "word gap" study I mentioned earlier in the book?[13] Having a device constantly on may increase your child's word gap.

[47] John, et al. 2021. "Association of screen time with parent-reported cognitive delay in preschool children of Kerala, India" *BMC Pediatrics.*
[48] Christakis, et al. 2009. "Audible television and decreased adult words, infant vocalizations, and conversational turns: A population-based study." *JAMA Pediatrics.*

Designate times and places as screen free

As a family, agree on a media use policy.[49] Mark certain times and places as screen free.

Put away gadgets and turn off the television during meals.[50] Research shows that mealtime screen use is associated with more eating problems, emotional and behavioral problems, and increased junk food intake.[51]

To help prevent sleep problems, turn off gadgets at least an hour before bedtime. Ideally, keep electronic devices out of the bedroom.[52]

Set a good example

Several research studies from various countries consistently show that parental screen time is one of the biggest factors influencing a child's screen time. This means kids of parents who have more screen time are more likely to have excess screen time as well.[53]

---

[49] "How to Make a Family Media Use Plan." https://www.healthychildren.org/English/family-life/Media/Pages/How-to-Make-a-Family-Media-Use-Plan.aspx.

[50] Martinot, et al. 2021. "Exposure to screens and children's language development in the EDEN mother-child cohort." *Scientific Reports.* This is a French study of 1,562 children age 2-6 years. In this research, overall daily screen time was not associated with scores in a language test. However, regardless of how much screen time a child got, having the television always on during family meals was associated with a lower verbal IQ for two-year-old kids.

[51] Jusiene, et al. 2019. "Screen use during meals among young children: Exploration of associated variables." *Medicina* (Kaunas).

[52] Hale, et al. 2019. "Youth screen media habits and sleep: Sleep-friendly screen-behavior recommendations for clinicians, educators, and parents." *Child and Adolescent Psychiatric Clinics of North America.*

[53] In addition to the 2021 Kaspersky study, "Raising the smartphone generation," earlier studies already showed links between screen use of parents and kids.

Arundell, et al. 2020. "Home-based screen time behaviors amongst youth and their parents: Familial typologies and their modifiable correlates." *BMC Public Health.*

Goncaves, et al. 2019. "Parental influences on screen time and weight status among preschool children from Brazil: A cross-sectional study." *International Journal of Behavior Nutrition and Physical Activity.*

Lauricella, et al. 2015. "Young children's screen time: The complex role of parent and child factors." *Journal of Applied Developmental Psychology.*

Limiting screen time will be good for your mental health too. Many researches have studied what is now known as "digital stress."[54] This is the stress that comes from being constantly connected.

The best time to limit your child's screen exposure is now. It's much easier to control the screen use of a toddler than to take it away from a child who's been put in front of a gadget since he was a baby. The longer your child gets excess screen time every day, the more difficult it will be for you to reduce it later on, because her brain will be used to the constant stimulation.

I often encounter parents whose kids have speech delay who say, "My biggest regret is giving my child so much screen time."

If you haven't introduced screen time yet, do what you can to keep to the screen time guidelines. It's much easier to not start, than to try to take away a gadget from a baby who's already used to it.

If, on the other hand, you feel your child is getting too much screen time, replace at least some of it with screen-free activities. Try to make whatever screen time she gets the kind that is slower paced.

I say this with empathy and without judgment. I understand how parenting can feel like fighting multiple battles every minute and how gadgets can give us the break we're desperate for. That's why this book is here to support you with alternatives, to help you avoid even bigger struggles in the future.

---

[54] These studies are summarized in Fischer, et al. 2021. "The Digital Stressors Scale: Development and validation of a new survey instrument to measure digital stress perceptions in the workplace context." *Frontiers in Psychology*. The Organization for Economic Cooperation and Development (OECD) also has a very interesting summary of the evidence in their report, "Children and Young People's Mental Health in the Digital Age." https://www.oecd.org/els/health-systems/Children-and-Young-People-Mental-Health-in-the-Digital-Age.pdf.

The good news? When parents learn the truth about screen time, many are finally motivated to put a stop to it. Yes, it's difficult. But for every single one of them, the effort was worth it.

If you have any concerns about the effect of screen time on your child's development, discuss it with your pediatrician.

Also, if you're finding it extremely difficult to limit the screen time of anyone in the family and you worry it may be an addiction already, simple willpower and "setting firm limits" may not be enough. Professional help may be needed.

Many people are surprised when they hear there's a specialty called addiction psychiatry. Before, these specialists used to deal mostly with drug and alcohol addiction. Today though, screen time addiction is increasingly becoming one of the most common reasons that patients—both kids and adults—consult with them.

CHAPTER 10

WHAT TO DO IF YOU'RE WORRIED YOUR CHILD MIGHT HAVE SPEECH DELAY

Bob and Belinda have a daughter, Brenda, who's eighteen months old.

Brenda is such a joy and delight. She's happy, cheerful, and sweet. She gives big smiles and hugs that never fail to melt the heart of anyone on the receiving end.

Belinda is worrying, though. At eighteen months, Brenda has not been able to say a single word. Not even mommy. Her older kids, Betty and Brad, were already talking when they were this age.

Their relatives have many different comments.

- *"Why isn't she talking yet?"*
- *"That's because you give her everything she wants. She's so spoiled!"*
- *"You're not teaching her! Enroll her in online classes and let her watch YouTube videos so she will learn."*
- *"Don't worry. It's because she's been stuck at home. Now that she can go out more, she'll be fine."*

Across the street, Dennis and Deidre have a son, Danny, who's two years old.

Danny has already memorized the alphabet and can count to twenty. He can name over twenty different animals and knows the types of dinosaurs. You can even show him the flags of some countries and he can name them.

Dennis and Deidre have their secret worries, however. He doesn't call them "Mommy" and "Daddy." He doesn't even look at them when they call him. When Danny wants something, he cries and they have to figure out what he wants. Sometimes, he will get Deidre's hand and pull her towards whatever it is that he wants. Danny doesn't respond to what they say—even simple things like, "Where's the ball?"

Once, Deidre summoned the courage to tell a friend about her worries. "Oh, that's normal!" her friend said. "Boys are really like that. Besides, he doesn't go out much and he's the only kid in the house. And just look at how smart he is! You're worrying over nothing."

I N THIS CHAPTER, we'll talk about what to do if you're worried your child might have speech delay. The specific steps may be different depending on where you're located, but here's the general process.

Developmental Surveillance and Screening by Your Pediatrician or Primary Care Physician[55]

Your pediatrician or family doctor will perform what we call developmental surveillance and screening.

In developmental surveillance, your doctor will interview you, as well as observe and examine your child. Your doctor does this at each well child visit—for example, when you bring your child to be vaccinated.

Compared with developmental surveillance which is done each time you visit your doctor, developmental screening is done at specific ages. In developmental screening, your doctor will perform a test that helps pick up developmental problems early on. The commonly used screening tests are quick to perform. Most of them can be answered with an interview with you or by asking you to fill out a questionnaire.

There are two kinds of tests that the American Academy of Pediatrics recommends during the toddler years.

The first test is the general developmental screen. These are recommended at nine months, eighteen months, and thirty months. Some of the most popular developmental screening tests are the Parental Evaluation of Developmental Status and the Ages and Stages Questionnaire.

The second type of test is what we call an autism-specific screen, the most common of which is the Modified Checklist for Autism in

---

[55] https://www.aap.org/en/patient-care/developmental-surveillance-and-screening-patient-care/.

Toddlers (MCHAT). If your doctor tells you to answer this, don't feel defensive and think that your doctor is labelling your child as possibly having autism. This test is recommended for *all* toddlers at eighteen and thirty months of age.

In addition to these, any time you have worries or concerns about your child's development, your pediatrician will do a screening test, even if it's not in the ages I mentioned above.

The purpose of screening is early detection. Screening does not mean diagnosis. For example, if your child is classified as "high risk" for autism based on the MCHAT, it's not the same as receiving a diagnosis of autism.

Evaluation by a Developmental and Behavioral Pediatrician

Depending on the results of developmental surveillance and screening, your doctor may decide to refer you for an evaluation by a developmental and behavioral pediatrician.

During the evaluation, the "dev peds," as they are called, will do an interview with you and review your child's medical and developmental history. She will also observe your child and do testing as needed. Many of the tests are done through play.

When the developmental pediatrician is conducting the test, it can be tempting to "help" your child by coaching or providing some cues, especially if you think it's a skill that your child has done at home. For example, if the doctor is asking about body parts, and you know your child has memorized, "Head Shoulders Knees and Toes," you may be tempted to sing or hum the song to help your child.

However, to be able to best help your child and get an accurate assessment, we need to keep the test as close to standardized conditions as possible. That's why, unless the doctor specifically instructs you to coach, it's better to simply observe what your child does. When the test is over, you may tell the doctor what your child can do at home so that this can be considered as well.

Sometimes, your doctor may not be able to give a diagnosis right away. For example, the first time you see your doctor, you may get a diagnosis of global developmental delay. Later on, the diagnosis may change to autism spectrum disorder. This does not mean that the first diagnosis was wrong, but it's evolving based on what we see.

Unlike, say COVID-19 where a positive PCR test means that you have a COVID-19 infection, there's no simple test that tells you the reason why a child has language delay. The process includes interviewing you, observing and examining your child (sometimes over a period of time), and doing additional tests if needed.

So it's not unusual if the initial assessment will be something like "receptive and expressive language delay," or "developmental language delay," without any clearer diagnosis. Diagnosing a developmental and behavioral disorder is a complex process!

Laboratory Testing

There's no one-size-fits-all testing plan. Some kids may need more tests, while others won't.

Even if your child had a normal hearing test as a baby, if there's speech delay, your doctor may decide to repeat it.

Your doctor may order an analysis of your child's chromosomes or other genetic tests. Depending whether or not your doctor suspects other medical problems, she may also order an EEG (electroencephalogram), metabolic tests, or other exams.

Intervention

Intervention often involves seeing a speech and language pathologist. Each child may be different in terms of how often and how long he will need therapy, so try not to compare your child's program with others.

Your doctor may also prescribe occupational therapy and other forms of therapy if needed. An early childhood education specialist may also be involved. Therapists, psychologists and teachers often also conduct their own evaluations.

The exact process for how to access intervention varies by country. In some countries, once you're enrolled in an early intervention program, you'll get a specific set of services that may include home visits by a parent educator. In others, you'll need to find and choose your own intervention team.

Each country will have its own licensing regulations. Be sure that the people you're paying to deliver your child's interventions are properly trained and licensed.

There are three things I want to emphasize when it comes to intervention. First, intervention is not something you leave only to the therapist or teacher. You and your family are the most important part of your child's intervention plan.

Even with a strong therapy program, unless you provide a language-rich environment at home, your child's progress may be limited. For example, you most likely won't see much improvement if your child continues to spend several hours a day glued to a gadget.

If you're a two-parent family living together, both parents need to be involved. Parents, daycare teachers, and others who help take care of the child will need to be on board.

Second, there are thousands—maybe even hundreds of thousands—of possible "interventions," "cures," or "programs" that are being marketed to parents. I often see parents who try one thing after another, or several simultaneously, because they want to "do everything possible" to help their child.

It's not possible to "do everything." Even if you had all the money in the world at your disposal, there simply aren't enough hours in a day to try every cure that pops up in your Facebook feed, try every "special diet" you read about, or follow every suggestion you hear. Doing this will take its toll on your sanity and your child's mental health.

That's why it's important to build your trusted team. This will include your pediatrician, developmental pediatrician, therapists, teachers, and other professionals working with your child. Find a team aligned with your values, and whom you can trust enough that you won't need to constantly Google everything they say. After all, for every single piece of advice you'll receive, there will always be websites that support it and others that say it's hogwash.

Third, every child is different. Don't compare your child's progress with that of another. Celebrate each win, no matter how small it may seem to you. When there are challenges or setbacks, don't lose hope.

A Final Note

Finally, here are five things I want you to remember, particularly when times get tough and you're feeling discouraged.

1. Your child is the same perfect child you gave birth to. When you first held your baby in your arms and gazed at him in wonder, you marveled at how perfect he is in every way. Your child's speech delay does not change any of that.

2. If your child fails to meet any developmental milestone, or if your child is diagnosed with speech delay, this does NOT mean you failed as a parent. Your worth as a parent is not attached in any way to when your child learns a skill or achieves a milestone.

3. Your family shouldn't fight or blame each other for your child's delay. It won't help your child. Even if your child isn't talking yet, he can sense the tension and this can lead to emotional issues.

4. Don't do it alone. It takes a village to raise a child. You need your "village." Your trusted team of professionals. Your loved ones. People you may hire to help you at home. Friends and other support systems. Choose people who truly help and empower you, and not toxic people who drain your hope and energy.

5. Take care of yourself too. Don't make your child your "project" to the point that you neglect yourself and stress out your child in the process. Your child needs you to be physically and mentally healthy. If you need professional help yourself, go for it. There's no shame in that.

You've got this! You are the best parent for your child. Don't doubt that. You're entrusted with this unique responsibility to bring out the best in your child—whatever her unique traits may be.

Dennis and Deidre brought Danny to see a developmental pediatrician. After interviewing them, observing Danny's behavior, and doing some tests, the pediatrician said that Danny had delays in his development.

As if that weren't shocking enough, she also said that Danny may be in the autism spectrum. She recommended starting therapy right away.

When Dennis and Deidre revealed this to some of their relatives, reactions were mixed.

- *"It's great that you know right away. Now you can get the help you need."*

- *"What?!! How dare the doctor say that Danny might have autism? She's just not used to seeing such smart kids. Get a second, third, and fourth opinion!"*

- *"That can't be right. I know all about autism from watching Rain Man. Danny is not Rain Man!"*

- *"Get these supplements and go on this diet. They're proven to cure kids with speech delay and autism!"*

This brought on even more confusion, on top of how they were already feeling about themselves and their own parenting skills.

Fortunately, they found a team that they could trust. Their pediatrician, developmental pediatrician, therapists and teachers worked together with them to help Danny. They spoke with their pediatrician and had reasonable discussions about what interventions to try.

Across the street, Brenda confided her worries to Bob. They brought these up with their pediatrician. After doing a screening test, the pediatrician recommended seeing a developmental pediatrician.

At first, Brenda's parents were crushed. Being told that their daughter might have speech delay felt like a huge blow to them as parents. They also wonder whether they're simply overreacting. Maybe it's better to wait and see whether Brenda will eventually start talking on her own or with the help of this app that promises to help kids learn to talk.

They decided to go ahead with the developmental pediatrics consult. Brenda received early intervention with a supportive speech therapist, who also taught them how to stimulate her language development at home.

It will take some time and the journey isn't perfect. But they receive valuable support from each other as well as from their doctors, therapists, and selected family members they've chosen to confide in.

Both couples started seeing improvements their kids' language skills. They're quite hopeful. They know that they shouldn't compare their kids' progress with that of other kids. Each improvement is a win to be celebrated.

NEXT STEPS

THANK YOU FOR going on this journey with me. We've gone through how language develops in your child, and what skills to expect at what age. We talked about practical ways to build your child's language and brain development.

I want you to experience the joy that comes with witnessing your child's daily wins and discoveries. With the powerful strategies of talking, playing and reading with your child, the *parenting magic wand* that you now have in your arsenal, and the many age-specific activities in this book, you're well on your way to helping your toddler learn to talk.

These strategies aren't just for the toddler years. As your child grows older, continue talking with her about school, friends, and anything she may be worried about. If you build the habit of having conversations and truly listening and responding to your child, you'll be more likely to weather stages such as the stormy teenage years.

Continue playing with your child beyond the toddler years. And even as your child grows older, books are a great way to have conversations and connect with your child.

By doing these, you give your child one of the best protective factors there is—a strong, connected, and responsive relationship with you. This sets up your child for success not just today, in learning to talk, but in every aspect of life in the future.

For updates and more resources to help you, go to toddlertalkingbook.com.

WHAT ARE WE DOING TO OUR KIDS?

We remove their outdoor spaces
And we hardly let them play
We confine them to concrete jungles
Where they stay cooped up all day.

And when with them we do go out
We don't visit nature that delights
But it's still to indoor spaces
Just with more noise and shiny lights.

We stop them from doing
What their brains are programmed to do
Like making a mess or touching things
Or exploring and climbing too.

We give them games and gadgets
We say these make them smarter
We're constantly glued to our phones
We're in the same room but not together.

We don't ask and we don't listen
How do they feel? Do they lack sleep?
We say they're spoiled or naughty
When they say no or shout or weep.

We tease and we provoke
Then we laugh at their reaction
And when they follow our example
We say it's insubordination.

We forget that kids imitate what we do
We scare and threaten so
We tell mom that she must toughen up
Because it's fear she needs to sow.

We dictate their every action
We don't let them decide
But when they resist and we get so tired
We give up and don't even guide.

Then when our kids misbehave, as they are bound to do
We don't understand; we don't bother asking
What's the real story? How can we help?
Instead we click our tongues and say, "This proves they need a spanking!"

Everyday that's what it's like
Until their brains now think it's true
That they really are so naughty
And do things that get to you.

We need to stop this cycle
Of criticizing and assuming
For if we try and help our kids
We can all experience healing.

Let's understand, connect, and communicate
Bring back play, go back to nature
Our kids will learn and grow and thrive
And we'll build a better future.

Victoria Ang-Nolasco, MD
2022-05-19

Author's Note: This poem is not meant to be a criticism of our parenting. Rather, it's my commentary on how our culture today can be toxic for both parents and kids.

DISCERNING PARENTING

POSITIVE PARENTING COACH +
DEVELOPMENTAL & BEHAVIORAL PEDIATRICIAN:
Victoria Ang-Nolasco, MD

For more parenting tips and inspiration,
listen to the Discerning Parenting podcast on
your favorite podcast app.

ABOUT THE AUTHOR

Dr. Victoria Ang-Nolasco is a developmental and behavioral pediatrician and parent of a young child. She has been a clinical associate professor of pediatrics and a university lecturer in brain psychology.

She also coaches parents on early childhood development, play, and positive parenting. It's her mission to empower parents of babies and toddlers with effective parenting strategies, so they parent with confidence and joy.

She is the host of the Discerning Parenting podcast and author of The Discerning Parent's Guide to Toddler Behavior: From Power Struggles to Connection.

To learn more and access the resources that come with this book, go to toddlertalkingbook.com.

www.ingramcontent.com/pod-product-compliance
Lightning Source LLC
Chambersburg PA
CBHW031155020426

42333CB00013B/672